milestones of
jazz

S
H
A
D

milestones of

jazz

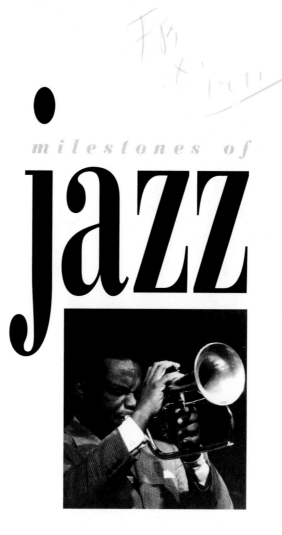

**A chronological history of jazz music
in photographs**

LINTON CHISWICK

CLB

"And I ask myself:

Are your fingers long enough to play
Old keys that are but echoes:
Is the silence strong enough
To carry back the music to its source
And back to you again? "

HART CRANE

Dedication:
To Karen, with love, always.

4972 *Milestones of Jazz*
This edition published in 1997 by CLB International,
a division of Quadrillion Publishing Limited,
Godalming, Surrey, England

Distributed in the U.S.A. by BHB International, Inc.
30 Edison Drive, Wayne, New Jersey 07470

© 1997 CLB International

Commissioning editor: Will Steeds
Copy editor: Ros Cocks
Designer: Justina Leitão
Picture research: David Redfern and Nancy White, Redferns The Music Picture Library, London
Production: Neil Randles, Ruth Arthur, Karen Staff
Index: Chris Bernstein
Color reproduction: Withers Litho, England

ISBN 1-85833-764-X

CONTENTS

FOREWORD

I have over the years been asked to write many forewords to jazz books but usually I refuse. It is a bit like being asked to supply a few pictures for an exhibition. You put a lot of effort into your own content but have no control over other people's input ...generally this is not very satisfactory.

I hear the cry, "But isn't this just another jazz book, so why are you writing about this one?" Well, I truly believe this book achieves what it sets out to do: to provide a clear overview of the main developments in jazz over the course of the 20th century. I was also very involved in the sourcing and final selection of the pictures used in this book. So I am delighted to be able to write these few words.

There is nothing revolutionary about *Milestones of Jazz*, but it really will provide all newcomers to jazz with a clear idea of who did what, when and with whom, explaining how jazz has developed over the years. Readers will be able to put any jazz they listen to into context after reading this book, and it will greatly assist them in finding out what they really like.

The photographs obviously play a crucial role in getting the story across in a book such as this. I have tried to get the very best pictures for the job – pictures that help tell the story, rather than "arty" pictures for "art's sake." My aim has been to source pictures that help show the story of jazz, and to try and find some pictures that have not been seen often before (if ever).

I have been fortunate enough to know some of the great jazz photographers, and there are some of the finest represented in this book. We have, for example, Bill Gottlieb's evocative images from the 1930s and 1940s, and Chuck Stewart's vibrating 1950s and 1960s images; we also have Duncan Schiedt's 1950s masterpieces, which are a sheer joy to me, and the book culminates with Danny Gignoux's impressions of the contemporary jazz scene.

Linton has written a great book which will be of interest to all jazz fans from the knowledgeable to the newcomer.

Enjoy!

David Redfern

INTRODUCTION

From humble roots to international art form in less than one hundred years, jazz has carved itself an heroic history. Even in its very earliest forms, it could demonstrate a fragile perfection – a flawless balance between message and medium in the music of, say, Louis Armstrong or Sidney Bechet, that set it apart from anything heard ever before.

Within these pages I have concentrated on the figures who have marked the music's course. The intention of this book was never to provide a comprehensive or exhaustive history of jazz. For every musician featured, there are another 30 whom I could have included, and five whom it broke my heart to omit. But by keeping the project to this length, I hope that it will suggest an overview of one of the 20th century's original arts – how it has mirrored and occasionally influenced the social changes taking place around it.

Jazz has held a special fascination for photographers. With the help of David Redfern, one of the world's leading jazz photographers, and Nancy White at Redferns The Music Picture Library, we have chosen pictures that are not only beautiful, but hopefully will give the newcomer a sense of the music itself. In many cases we have rejected the obvious choice, and sought images that have rarely been seen before – something that should make this book attractive to the inveterate jazz fan too.

If I hadn't been listening to a certain radio station at a certain time on a certain day, I may never have known the extraordinary power contained in this music – and my life would be very different. But a chance encounter with tenor saxophonist John Coltrane, driving relentlessly forward through the chord changes of *Cousin Mary*, created an energy that was almost tangible. Since then I have had the good fortune of meeting a few of the architects of jazz, and learning at first hand about some of the personalities behind the music. A few of them are quoted within these pages.

If this book encourages people to dip into the jazz legacy themselves, then it is doing the right thing.

Linton D. Chiswick

1902 1928
NEW ORLEANS
TO NEW YORK

MAX JONES FILES

It is 1902. Among the frenetic nightlife of one of America's liveliest ports – where the daily influx of merchant sailors mixes with the local black, Creole and white populations, in search of entertainment – an unknown black 25-year-old cornet player called Buddy Bolden blows a startling call to arms. He is marking the dawn of the 20th century's greatest original art form. ▶

Right: Silver-haired soprano genius, Sidney Bechet. ●
Above: Fine, Memphis-born trumpeter Johnny Dunn recorded with Jelly Roll Morton in the late 1920s. ●

WILLIAM GOTTLIEB

O f course, Bolden himself has no idea that he has achieved something of so much significance. But the uniquely swinging sound that emanates from the bell of his horn and – if legend is to be believed – carries out of New Orleans and right across the State line, stopping people in their tracks like a bolt from the blue, will be heard again. For the Bolden chromosome in the trumpet gene pool will reappear hidden in Roy Eldridge's attack in the 1940s; it will lie deep in Clifford Brown's fire and momentum in the 1950s. Nor would Bolden have imagined in his wildest dreams that, in the 1980s, more than half a century after his death, another New Orleans trumpeter – Wynton Marsalis – would be playing impressions of the Bolden style in front of paying audiences.

Buddy Bolden is considered by many to be the very first jazz musician, and he was almost certainly the first great jazz cornet player. Yet he never recorded, and anyone still alive who might have heard him would be stretching their memories to provide a description of his style.

The early years of the century were the dark days of jazz prehistory – they survive today only as a confused but fascinating mixture of fact and conjecture, in which myth and reality continue to battle it out for supremacy. Certainly, given that the source and processes of human creativity are unpredictable, the genesis of a complex new art form can never be explained by means of a simple formula, or summarized in a neat chronological history. But there are some things we do know about the earliest days of jazz.

The new jazz music had three important antecedents. There was the marching band tradition of German and Italian origin which, in the black communities, took on a kind of African-style, ceremonial status. There was ragtime piano (from "ragged time," describing the combination of *tempo di marcia* left hand and syncopated right – a lively piano style, popular today). Lastly there was the blues: a powerful, vocal-based folk music, with its roots in the African-American slave era and African music itself.

By the turn of the century each of these musical styles existed across the American South and Midwest. The "father" of ragtime, Scott Joplin, who in 1897 set the rag style with the publication of *Original Rags*, was based in Sedalia, Missouri. It was, however, almost exclusively New Orleans that spawned the first generation of jazz musicians. With its Mississippi River steamship trade and healthy local economy, it was known as a boom town. It had an unusually progressive – for the South, at least – attitude toward its black populace. While elsewhere the last vestiges of African culture had been either outlawed or driven underground and disguised, New Orleans encouraged the continued celebration of African tradition. There was dancing and music regularly in its Congo Square. In the middle-class Creole district, pale-skinned blacks learned to read and play orchestral and chamber music.

Ironically, the turning of the political tide in the 1890s, when New Orleans' booming economy encouraged an influx of whites, may have been the biggest catalyst in the creation of the powerful, new black art form. For, when the segregationist White League applied pressure on blacks and Creoles to move into the same districts together, the result was an inevitable cross-fertilization between the two groups. The Creoles' technical prowess and theoretical knowledge combined with

Above: Buddy Bolden – the first New Orleans cornet king, and the man commonly considered the father of jazz. ●

Right: An advanced, musically literate pianist, composer and bandleader, Jelly Roll Morton used his Red Hot Peppers to make some of the most sophisticated jazz sounds of the 1920s. ●

the improvisational tricks and syncopation of the black marching band musicians.

Skillful Creole clarinetists, powerful marching band brass players and drummers, blues banjo players and guitarists, and ragtime pianists all began playing a music with a new sound. Taking the structure of ragtime and applying it to this small group lineup, the early jazz musicians spread out the 2/4 march beat to a mellower, more swinging 4/4, and the new music was more or less born.

When did this happen? Earwitnesses claim to have heard Buddy Bolden first playing a music that fits this description in 1902. New Orleans-born pianist and composer Jelly Roll Morton – one of the most successful bandleaders of the 1920s – claimed in interviews to have invented jazz single-handedly by applying the 4/4 meter to ragtime in... 1902. So 1902 will do as well as any other date, as a hypothetical starting-point for jazz history.

Without amplification, neither the guitar nor the slightly more cutting banjo could operate efficiently as a melodic instrument next to the noisy brass instruments. As a result, guitarists/banjo players tended to work mainly as rhythm section players, strumming and highlighting the chords alongside the bass. Clarinetists were often the most musically advanced musicians in early jazz due to their Creole training in the slick social dance and chamber groups of downtown New Orleans. They played a demanding role, highlighting the chords and ornamenting the melody with a constant commentary of intricate arpeggios and scales. But the kings of early jazz were the cornet and trumpet men. It was their job to carry, and improvise on, the melody. The best

trumpeters cut through with a clear, melodic and rhythmically inventive line, confidently leading the whole ensemble from the front.

Buddy Bolden was followed by a line of gifted, New Orleans-born cornet players and trumpeters: bandleaders who directed jazz through its earliest stages. Freddie Keppard, born in 1890, led a jazz group on a tour to both American coasts in the years before the First World War. By the time he came to record, however, his music had changed significantly from those early New Orleans days.

MICHAEL OCHS ARCHIVES

Buddy Petit inherited the crown, co-leading one of New Orleans' celebrated early jazz groups after Keppard had joined the massive black migration of the period to settle in Chicago. Petit remained in New Orleans and never got to record. Like Bolden, his reputation rests on a host of earwitness testimonies.

King Oliver, a powerful cornet player with all

New Orleans-born pianist and composer Jelly Roll Morton claimed to have invented jazz single-handedly.

the necessary leadership attributes, left for Chicago at the beginning of the 1920s and, once there, formed one of the most important bands of the period. Remembering a young, gifted player he had stumbled across in New Orleans, Oliver sent for him, so bringing to the attention of the public, for the very first time, the man who would come to encapsulate the New Orleans trumpet tradition for evermore: Louis Armstrong.

As the musicians migrated to the North, their music began to grow significantly in popularity, its commercial potential dawning on those holding the purse strings. Thus, the very first jazz recording was by a white band: a clever, PR-friendly amalgam called the Original Dixieland Jazz Band, who claimed to have invented the music themselves. They said they could not read music, but their records reveal very little improvisation.

What they played was really a kind of novelty music, complete with comical barnyard sound effects, closer perhaps to the minstrel tradition than the genesis of jazz. However, their *Livery Stable Blues* (also known as *Barnyard Blues*), recorded in 1917, was a big – if brief – hit with the public. The band then vanished into recording history during the mid-1920s. Misleading and moderately skilled though the Original Dixieland Jazz Band might have been, it had some beneficial effects on the early course of jazz history: awakening the recording world to jazz, and inspiring a new generation of gifted white musicians.

The first recording of black jazz dates from 1922, when trombonist Kid Ory – a former New Orleans luminary who had already worked with King Oliver but was at the time touring the West Coast – cut a series of sides for the California-based Sunshine label. But it was in 1923 when black jazz and the recording industry really got together. In that one year, Freddie Keppard, King Oliver, Louis Armstrong, Jelly Roll Morton, Creole clarinet virtuoso Sidney Bechet, pianist Clarence Williams and jazz/blues vocal legend Bessie Smith all made their first recordings.

King Oliver's Chicago recordings are often considered the blueprint for the "authentic New Orleans style." These intense polyphonic performances are the first recorded jazz masterpieces – flawless musical miniatures that resonate like distant gems despite the scratchy, rough recording quality. Since Oliver's days in New Orleans, it is likely that jazz had acquired some sophistication in its presentation; listeners therefore cannot take it as given that these recordings replicate the New Orleans sound authentically. Although some historians have suggested that, as Oliver was playing in a consciously old-fashioned manner, the sides do give us a good idea of how the style sounded. Whatever the position of the music at the time, the quality and antique beauty of this intricate, almost baroque music is undeniable.

Louis Armstrong left Oliver's band toward the end of 1923 to accept a trumpet job in New York. Already noted for his strength and invention as a lead player, over the next few years he transformed the leader's role in jazz, using bands as vehicles for a more solo-oriented approach. In the mid-1920s, he led a series of bands known as the Hot Fives and Hot Sevens (many musicians

Already noted for his strength and invention as a leading player, Louis Armstrong transformed the leader's role in jazz, using bands as vehicles for a more solo-oriented approach.

were poached from Oliver) in one of the most prolific recording periods any jazz musician has ever achieved. Although Armstrong grew in popularity throughout his career, many jazz purists believe that it was at this time that the artist was at his peak. There is no doubt that tracks such as *Hotter Than That* and *West End Blues*, with its ferociously swinging, virtuoso blast of an introduction, represented an entirely new era in the music and an extraordinary improviser finding his voice.

The new "hot" music, already being known as "jazz," found an enthusiastic, if not always healthy, following in the Northern cities. With prohibition turning the art of socializing into a complex, clandestine affair and filling the boot-leggers' and mobsters' pockets just as fast as the populace could drink, the clubs and speakeasies used entertainment to win trade. For a while, the new generation of musicians found plenty of work, at least.

In Chicago, the first Northern city adopted by the exiled New Orleans crowd, a generation of white musicians became entranced by the new sound. At first, cruder outfits such as the New Orleans Rhythm Kings and the Original Memphis Five – encouraged mainly by the success of the Original Dixieland Jazz Band – set out to cash in on this latest trend.

However, a young, gifted cornet player called Bix Beiderbecke, who had already heard New Orleans musicians, including Armstrong and Oliver, playing on the Mississippi steamboats that passed through his Iowa home town of Davenport, managed to distill the essence of the music while retaining his own clean, almost classical tone. Moving to Chicago, he took the opportunity to listen to what were an unlikely series of musical heroes for a middle-class, Midwestern white boy. He used what he had learned to turn some Original Dixieland Jazz Band songs into recordings of a profundity and beauty of which they could not even have dreamed.

At the end of the 1920s the white jazz scene exploded. A loose collective of musicians was formed, with Beiderbecke at the center. It featured guitarist Eddie Condon, trumpeter Jimmy McPartland, saxophonist Bud Freeman, drummer Gene Krupa, and clarinetist and soon-to-be jazz legend Benny Goodman. They became known as the Austin High School Gang, and played a cooler-sounding music than their black counterparts. But, with the exception of Beiderbecke himself, whose famous thirst would make him an early casualty of the musician's lifestyle, these were musicians whose greatest achievements were yet to come.

Just before the Wall Street Crash, Chicago announced an unprecedented, no-nonsense policy against the gangsters and breakers of the alcohol prohibition, which might have delighted the guardians of the city's moral values, but did nothing to make life easier for the new generation of jazz musicians. Moving East to New York City, Condon and his pals would immortalize the sound of "Chicago jazz" in the forthcoming decades. Already, however, the froth was visible on a new wave of noisy and exciting jazz activity. America braced itself for the coming of the big band.

S.A. JAZZ MEMORIES

Above: Cornetist Bix Beiderbecke was the most gifted of the first generation of white jazz musicians. ●

Left: He is "The King of the Trumpet," heading an authentic New Orleans program in California. But they are uncertain how to spell his name. ●

17

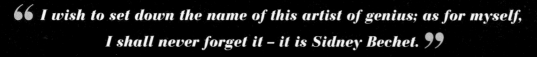

> **_I wish to set down the name of this artist of genius; as for myself,
> I shall never forget it – it is Sidney Bechet._**

ERNEST ANSERMET

NEW ORLEANS: THE FIRST GENERATION

S.A. JAZZ MEMORIES

Left: A young Jelly Roll Morton, looking grand at the grand piano. Morton claimed to have invented jazz in 1902. ●

Left inset: Sidney Bechet. ●

Above: Cornetist King Oliver made some of the finest recordings of the early 1920s, and discovered the young Louis Armstrong. ●

Out of the hectic nightlife of turn-of-the-century New Orleans, a handful of black musicians pulled together the musical influences that surrounded them, to create what would be America's most significant single contribution to the cultural world. No-one could have guessed that this was the start of a phenomenally fast-moving art form, one that would develop from folk to abstraction in less than a century.

The New Orleans jazz blueprint was a beautiful music. Quite unlike the sometimes crude and brash copies that would come later, the original, classic jazz sound relied on a delicate balance – an edgy fragility that came with "making music in the moment." This sound would characterize much of the century's best jazz.

Listening to these scratchy, lo-fi recordings today – King Oliver's glittering, antique beauty, Louis Armstrong's powerful affirmations of life – and looking at the faces of the men and women who made them, there is an odd kind of history revealed. It is a history that is tantalizingly out of reach, and yet, at the same time, there, to dip into, on hundreds of records and photographs.

Right: Commercial recording did not come in time for cornetist Buddy Bolden (born *probably* on September 6, 1877), yet he is still considered New Orleans' first great jazz musician. This figure — surrounded by myth and hyperbole — was a mischievous, subversive musician who caused a virtual rebellion in 1898 by playing *Home, Sweet Home* to soldiers as they left to fight in the Spanish-American War. He packed a marvelous, powerful punch on his instrument, but his wild lifestyle saw him tragically committed to a mental institution at the age of 29. ●

Right: Cornetist Freddie Keppard had an authentic New Orleans marching band training. His tough, *staccato* style suggested ragtime roots. Only rough-and-ready recordings survive, but he was esteemed by his contemporaries. ●

Right: The third of New Orleans' cornet kings, Buddy Petit *(shown standing, center)* never recorded, but played in his home town until his death in 1931. Standing to Petit's left is brilliant New Orleans clarinetist Edmond Hall. ●

Right: Bessie Smith – "the Empress of the Blues." Born in Tennessee in 1894, Bessie Smith was the creative force, along with her teacher Ma Rainey, behind the development of "classic blues." Before Rainey and Smith, the blues had been purely a folk music, like the worksong, the field holler, and the spiritual. Rainey and Smith gave the music a commercial future, collaborating with jazz musicians on the vaudeville circuit to create a more defined structure. Smith recorded in 1923, along with the first wave of black recording artists, and quickly achieved a vast and enthusiastic following. She excelled at her art, singing with the depth and crystal-clear diction of a fine actress, the unstoppable swing of the cornet kings, and often specializing in risqué, sexually explicit lyrics. She recorded with some of the finest jazz musicians of the period, including pianists Clarence Williams and James P. Johnson, and made a series of classic recordings with Louis Armstrong. A consistently creative and musical performer, she was still performing and recording when a car accident brought her career to a premature halt in 1937. ●

MICHAEL OCHS ARCHIVES

S.A. JAZZ MÉMORIES

S.A. JAZZ MÉMORIES

Above: Joe "King" Oliver *(pictured standing at the back)* was born in May, 1885. A powerful, bluesy improviser, he was one of the original New Orleans cornet kings. Leading his superb Creole Jazz Band, featuring Louis Armstrong on second cornet, he played a legendary residency at Chicago's Lincoln Gardens and, in 1923, recorded some of the very finest examples of early jazz. Armstrong's first-ever recorded trumpet solo can be heard on the famous *Chimes Blues*. ●

MICHAEL OCHS ARCHIVES

S.A. JAZZ MEMORIES

S.A. JAZZ MEMORIES

BOTTOM ROW: DAVE BENNETT FILES

Above: "Baby" Dodds worked with Freddie Keppard and Jelly Roll Morton, and played in King Oliver's classic Creole Jazz Band. ●

Above: Baby's brother Johnny Dodds played tough, bluesy clarinet with the best exiled New Orleans bands, including King Oliver's. ●

Above: Pianist and composer Lil Hardin, another original member of Oliver's Creole Jazz Band, became Lil Armstrong in 1924. ●

S.A. JAZZ MEMORIES

WILLIAM GOTTLIEB

Left: To this day, Louis Armstrong is an iconic figure, synonymous with jazz. Born in New Orleans sometime at the beginning of the century (Armstrong's own claims that his birthday was July 4, 1900, should be taken in the spirit in which they were made), he learned the bugle and the cornet while at the Colored Waifs' Home. Fellow cornetist King Oliver took Armstrong under his wing, and in Chicago in the early 1920s, they made history as one of the most dynamic pairings in jazz.

Armstrong's own Hot Fives and Hot Sevens recordings of the mid-1920s include some of the first jazz masterpieces. His rich, brassy tone, massive swing and subtle, finely-tuned phrasing revealed an improviser miles ahead of any brass player around. In the 1930s he fronted big bands, by then playing trumpet exclusively; he also placed more emphasis on his unorthodox but popular singing style. But he sounded out of step with the swing era, and it was not until the creation of the All Stars small groups that he found a suitable setting from which he could work really well. Armstrong toured with different versions of the All Stars until his death in 1971, playing music that ranged from fast-moving Dixieland to saccharine pop.

Armstrong has become an oddly controversial figure, criticized for his clowning and accused of "Uncle Tomming" in his entertainment of white audiences. Many critics failed to see the musician within the social context from which he was born. Armstrong himself never separated his role as "musician" from his role as "entertainer," and was most happy when he could perform both. ●

MILESTONES:

S. BRUNSON CAMPBELL
IN HIS OWN WORDS

S. Brunson Campbell was Scott Joplin's only white pupil, and became known as "the Ragtime Kid." His words illustrate the emphasis on originality and personality that jazz would inherit from the ragtime piano scene.

"It was Scott Joplin over at Sedalia who set the true ragtime pattern in 1897 with Original Rags. *If that rag did not convince the critics that Joplin was the 'ragtime master,' then his next did, for it was his famous* Maple Leaf Rag *of 1899.*

But none of the original pianists played ragtime the way it was written. They played their own style. Some played march time, fast time, slow time, and some played ragtime blues style. But none of them lost the melody; and if you knew the player and heard him a block away you could name him by his ragtime style.

Scott Joplin named me the 'Ragtime Kid' after he had taught me to play his first four rags, and as I was leaving him in Sedalia to return to my home in Kansas he gave me a bright, new, shiny half-dollar and drew my attention to the date on it. 'Kid,' he said, 'This half-dollar is dated 1897, the year I wrote my first rag. Carry it for good luck, and as you go through life it will always be a reminder of your early ragtime days here at Sedalia.'"

MICHAEL OCHS ARCHIVES

Above and Right: Sidney Bechet's rich, sumptuous and intense, virtuoso soprano saxophone is without doubt one of the most exciting sounds in the history of New Orleans jazz. Bechet spent his teens playing with King Oliver and Freddie Keppard but, one of jazz's great explorers, he took off as soon as he had the opportunity, traveling to Europe, and even playing for the King of England. Notoriously wild, he was deported after he reputedly punched a prostitute, and then spent a brief time in New York recording with, among others, Louis Armstrong and Clarence Williams. But it was not long before Bechet was on the go again, touring across Europe and even Russia, before settling in Paris. He spent a year in prison following a shooting incident, during which time his hair turned gray, even though he was only in his mid-30s. When he returned to New York, this gray-haired, avuncular but hugely energetic reeds virtuoso was received by the burgeoning New Orleans jazz revivalist movement as a kind of figurehead. Bechet, perhaps compensating for having spent most of the 1920s abroad, relished the role. ●

MAX JONES FILES

MICHAEL OCHS ARCHIVES

Above: A fine pianist and important bandleader, Jelly Roll Morton spent the 1920s redefining the relationship between composition and improvisation. The best of his Red Hot Peppers recordings from this period, including *Grandfather's Spells* and *Original Jelly Roll Blues*, feature sophisticated structures and a well-rehearsed band. ●

MICHAEL OCHS ARCHIVES

Above: Prolific New Orleans trombonist Kid Ory became the first black jazz recording artist in 1922, when he cut his famous Sunshine sides in Los Angeles. He recorded with Oliver, Morton and Armstrong and, except for a spell spent working on a chicken farm, continued playing right through to the late 1960s. He died in 1973. ●

Above: The Original Dixieland Jazz Band – a five-piece, all-white band – was quick to seize upon the commercial potential of jazz, and even claimed to have invented the music. Their 1917 hit *Livery Stable Blues* (otherwise known as *Barnyard Blues*) is commonly considered the first jazz record. They made a crude, slapstick sound, but helped spread the jazz word, inspiring other white musicians, including talented improvisers such as Bix Beiderbecke. ●

Left: Resident in Chicago during the 1920s, the New Orleans Rhythm Kings played black music without claiming it as their own, and also influenced the young Bix Beiderbecke. ●

Left: One of five musical sons of a marching band clarinetist, Edmond Hall performed around New Orleans in the 1920s, including a spell with early cornet king Buddy Petit. It was in the 1940s that he made his reputation, recording with Eddie Condon, and joining, in the 1950s, Louis Armstrong's All Stars. By then, Hall's style had developed into a brilliant combination of bluesy New Orleans clarinet and the melodic craft of the swing players. Recommended recordings include a series of unusual quartet dates from 1941, featuring Meade Lux Lewis on celeste and Charlie Christian on acoustic guitar. ●

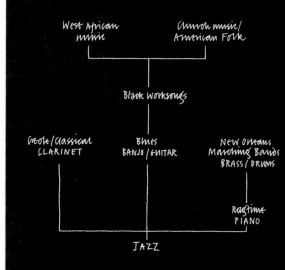

West African music

Church music/ American Folk

Black worksongs

Creole/Classical CLARINET

Blues BANJO/GUITAR

NEW Orleans Marching Bands BRASS/DRUMS

Ragtime PIANO

JAZZ

Above: Lush New Orleans clarinetist Barney Bigard played with King Oliver, Duke Ellington and Louis Armstrong. ●

Above: One of the most sophisticated of New Orleans clarinetists, Jimmie Noone *(seated center)* influenced swing players like Benny Goodman. ●

Above: New Orleans clarinetist Albert Nicholas enjoyed a long career, working with Buddy Petit in his teens and touring until 1973. ●

Many factors combined to create the perfect environment for the birth of jazz; but a few of its musical antecedents were clear for anyone to hear. The blues tradition lent the guitar; the Creole tradition, the clarinet; the brass came from the marching band; and the piano from its ragtime relative.

Above: A prolific drummer, Zutty Singleton recorded with Louis Armstrong and Jelly Roll Morton in the 1920s, and continued to work until 1970. ●

Above: New Orleans trumpeter Bunk Johnson claimed to have worked with Buddy Bolden in the 1890s. ●

Above: One of the last great New Orleans trumpeters of the 1920s, Henry "Red" Allen had a virtuoso style and could sound very similar to Armstrong. ●

> 66 *On bus or train rides, when I was with Ed [Condon], he'd get his guitar out. You should hear some of the gorgeous chords he played.* 99
>
> WILD BILL DAVISON, 1955

MIGRATION

JACK TEAGARDEN AND HIS BAND
APPEARING AT THE BLACKHAWK CAFE

S.A. JAZZ MEMORIES

I f jazz was born in New Orleans, it found its second home in Chicago. Many of the early jazz movement's key movers and shakers relocated to the Windy City, partly due to the clean-up, in 1917, of New Orleans' famous red-light district. There was also a continuing African-American migration North from the Southern states.

Ironically, the next time the moral guardians of America were to influence the course of jazz history, it was to work indirectly in the music's favor. With the Volstead Act of 1920, America became an alcohol-free zone …in theory. In practice, the cities went on a binge, and speakeasy owners turned to musicians in an attempt to draw customers away from the competition.

Black jazz made a momentous impression on Chicago's white musicians, creating a new generation of improvisers who began playing their own hard-swinging version of New Orleans jazz. A number of those belonging to this first wave of white Chicago jazz musicians would reappear in the 1930s, as the leaders of the new big band era.

Left: Wit, raconteur and extraordinary rhythm guitarist, Eddie Condon. ●

Above: Brilliant trombonist and vocalist Jack Teagarden, one of the first generation of white jazz musicians. ●

Right: Pee Wee Russell's long, mournful face perfectly expressed his often emotionally disarming clarinet style. A collaborator in the 1920s with Jack Teagarden, Frankie Trumbauer and Bix Beiderbecke, he would spend most of his career playing Dixieland jazz, while developing an idiosyncratic and highly personal approach. He was a famously heavy drinker which, combined with his musical eccentricity, sometimes led people to overlook the inquiring musical mind behind his odd approach to the instrument. The fact that he played with leaders as diverse as Louis Armstrong, Eddie Condon and Thelonious Monk should be seen as a testimony to his remarkable talent. ●

WILLIAM GOTTLIEB

Above: The first great jazz guitarist, Philadelphia-born Eddie Lang took advantage of new recording techniques to establish the guitar as a "lead" instrument, recording with violinist Joe Venuti, blues guitarist Lonnie Johnson and cornetist King Oliver. ●

Above: Guitarist and vocalist Lonnie Johnson's duets with Eddie Lang remain a high point in the history of jazz guitar. A skillful musician, Johnson also collaborated with Louis Armstrong, King Oliver and Duke Ellington. ●

Above: Trombonist and vocalist Jack Teagarden was so fine a technician that even the great trombonist Tommy Dorsey refused to solo alongside him. He recorded with Benny Goodman, and collaborated with Louis Armstrong. ●

S.A. JAZZ MEMORIES

Above: A bright and incisive, Bix Beiderbecke-influenced cornetist, Red Nichols led a series of prolifically recorded bands known as the Five Pennies, defining the strident white jazz sound of the late 1920s. The Five Pennies variously featured the finest up-and-coming musicians of the period, including Miff Mole, Eddie Lang, Pee Wee Russell, Jimmy Dorsey, Joe Venuti, Jack Teagarden, Artie Shaw and Benny Goodman. ●

MAX JONES FILES

Left: Hard-swinging violinist Joe Venuti, whose immortal collaboration with guitarist Eddie Lang prefigured the work of Reinhardt and Grappelli. ●

Right: Frankie Trumbauer *(at the back)*, a swinging saxophonist and regular collaborator with Bix Beiderbecke. ●

S.A. JAZZ MEMORIES

MILESTONES:
NEW ORLEANS JAZZ INSTRUMENTS

Cornet/Trumpet: Whether it was the thinner, more cutting cornet, or the richer and more versatile trumpet, this was the power bass in early jazz. The New Orleans cornet kings carried the melody to the people, using a host of vocal-style techniques — smears and growls — to add emotion to the melodic line.

Trombone: With neither the bite nor the articulation of the trumpet, the unique *glissando* potential of the slide trombone was used to provide a simplified, robust "second opinion."

Reeds: New Orleans' virtuoso clarinetists played an energetic jazz role, weaving between the simpler trumpet and trombone lines with nimble arpeggios and bluesy bent notes. Sidney Bechet, the most gifted of all New Orleans reedsmen, introduced the soprano saxophone as an alternative to the clarinet, and took advantage of its bigger, more intense sound.

Piano: Pianists had most influence as composers or bandleaders (e.g. Clarence Williams and Jelly Roll Morton). Playing a rag-style accompaniment throughout, they saved their best moments for the occasional two-bar break.

Guitar/Banjo: Resting somewhere between bass and piano, the stringsmen strummed a simple chordal accompaniment, often contributing to the swing and syncopation by placing the emphasis on the off-beats 2 & 4. The banjo, better able to cut through the noisy brass in these pre-amplification days, proved more popular.

Bass: Early jazz often favored the tuba ("brass bass") over the string bass, for practical reasons of volume, but you could expect to hear either in the New Orleans jazz band. The bass would play two beats to the bar, highlighting the roots of the chords.

Drums: The bass drum and the hi-hat cymbals were central to the early jazz drummer's style. In fact, New Orleans veterans such as Sidney Bechet would complain in years to come that their young drummers could not play the bass drum loud enough.

S.A. JAZZ MÉMORIES

This page: There are few sounds more beautiful or immediately electrifying than the fresh and burnished cry of Bix Beiderbecke's cornet. A vibrant, vigorous and yet fragile sound (described by Eddie Condon as "like a girl saying 'yes'"), it lacked the throatiness of King Oliver or the punchy virtuosity of Armstrong, but more than compensated with an utterly original cool swing and lyricism. Beiderbecke was a genius.

Born in Davenport, Iowa, in 1903, to a stolidly middle-class but musical family of German extraction, he was soon kicking against local constraints, compulsively playing records by the Original Dixieland Jazz Band, and going out to hear black New Orleans originals such as King Oliver and Louis Armstrong as they passed through Davenport on the riverboats. By 1923, he was playing his own jaunty version of the music, first with the now famous Wolverine Orchestra, then with a series of top dance bands and, in the late 1920s, his own group. Bix Beiderbecke liked to smoke a joint, but he liked to drink ridiculous quantities of prohibited liquor even more. He died in August 1931.

We are left with a legacy of glorious recordings — records such as *At the Jazz Band Ball*, *Sorry* and *Jazz Me Blues* (all recorded in 1927 by Bix Beiderbecke and his Gang), in which Beiderbecke's humorous, passionate personality shines through, encouraging the romantic legend that has grown up around him. ●

Right: Eddie Condon's four-stringed guitar was derived from the banjo he had played early in his career. One of the key players in the "Chicago jazz" style, he worked with Bix Beiderbecke and Bud Freeman in the late 1920s, and moved to New York in 1928 where, for four decades, he led bands featuring some of the boldest and brassiest Dixieland musicians around, including Wild Bill Davison, Jack Teagarden, Max Kaminsky and Pee Wee Russell. Condon was an irrepressible enthusiast who kept the music going through thick and thin, operating as nightclub owner and promoter as well as bandleader. Famous for his heavy drinking and sharp wit (his hangover cure reputedly began, "Take the juice of two quarts of whiskey…"), Condon was one of the great personalities of jazz. ●

CHUCK STEWART

MAX JONES FILES

MAX JONES FILES

Right: A member of the Austin High School Gang and a fine tenor saxophonist, Bud Freeman was a rare early rival to tenor giant Coleman Hawkins. ●

Left: Adrian Rollini played the hefty bass saxophone with the great Bix Beiderbecke. He is pictured here at the piano, with pianist Teddy Wilson standing behind. ●

S.A. JAZZ MEMORIES

WILLIAM GOTTLIEB

Far left: Drummer Cozy Cole began working as the swing era broke, but recorded his best work in small groups, including Louis Armstrong's All Stars. ●

Left: Clarinetist Pee Wee Russell, trumpeter Muggsy Spanier, trombonist Miff Mole and friend, outside Nick's – New York City's home of Dixieland. ●

S.A. JAZZ MEMORIES

S.A. JAZZ MÉMORIES

THE CLARINETISTS

THE CLARINET TRADITION

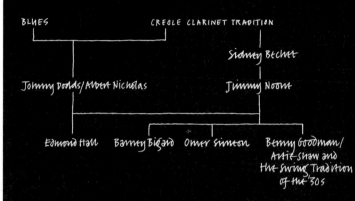

The clarinetists of early jazz were often the

most "schooled" players, many of them

trained by respected Creole musicians such as

Lorenzo Tio Junior or Alphonse Picou.

Johnny Dodds and Albert Nicholas gave the

intricate Creole style a rough, bluesy edge,

and influenced the brilliant Edmond Hall.

Virtuosi such as Sidney Bechet and

Jimmie Noone, meanwhile, were important in

the creation of what would become

the swing clarinet style.

Left and Above: Even by the mid-1920s, the seeds of the big band era were being sown. A young chemistry graduate called Fletcher Henderson had teamed up with conservatory-educated arranger Don Redman, and was leading an innovative band that combined the extended lineup of the dance orchestras with "hot" jazz trumpet solos (at first, by the great Louis Armstrong). By the end of the decade, the Fletcher Henderson Orchestra was New York's most popular dance band, setting the scene for the mighty swing machines that were to follow. ●

1928 1958

MAX JONES FILES

SWING TO BOP

Jazz history moves fast. By the mid-1920s, the classic New Orleans sound was already a thing of the past. The white population of Chicago was enjoying its own brassy and robust version of the New Orleans music, and King Oliver was still playing it – possibly tapping into an early form of the nostalgia market. But Oliver's young protégé Louis Armstrong, and even Jelly Roll Morton, were experimenting with larger formats and tighter, more formalized music. ▶

Right: Bop architects Thelonious Monk and Howard McGhee. ●
Above: Vibraphonist Lionel Hampton, with Duke Ellington and Louis Armstrong. ●

WILLIAM GOTTLIEB

This was the beginning of an interesting formative period – the classic jazz era was over, but the swing era was yet to begin. In New York, black middle-class college graduates, with little experience of the lusty, blues-infused polyphony of New Orleans jazz, were attracted by the increasing financial rewards and glamour associated with the new record industry and dance band scene. When Louis Armstrong left King Oliver, the first thing he did was travel to New York to take up a job with Fletcher Henderson, a young chemistry graduate and big band leader. Henderson was looking for a "hot" soloist to spice up what was in other respects a fairly pedestrian outfit. Armstrong briefly blew some life into the band, before leaving to pursue his own career as a leader.

Henderson, with innovative arrangers Don Redman and Benny Carter, would struggle through the thick of the mid-1920s to the thin of the post-Depression 1930s, planting the seeds of the swing era. The Fletcher Henderson Orchestra, resident at New York's prestigious Roseland Ballroom, was by 1926 New York's premier big band. Young black music fans, banned from entering the building, would huddle outside the back windows to listen.

During the same year, the massive Savoy Ballroom was built on Lennox Avenue, stretching a whole block between 140th and 141st Streets. By the early 1930s, a powerful drummer and bandleader called Chick Webb would become firmly ensconced there. His Savoy Orchestra

MAX JONES FILES

confidently took on all newcomers, keeping the Lindyhoppers on their toes, and marking the very eve of the swing era.

In the meantime, an urbane and good-looking Washingtonian named Edward Kennedy Ellington, and nicknamed "Duke" after his cultivated manner, had arrived in New York. Playing an intelligent, carefully arranged music that incorporated blues and vocal elements from New Orleans jazz into a lush and extravagant sound, he took over a residency at Harlem's prestigious Cotton Club, and set about writing the sound-track to the Harlem Renaissance. Promoters coined the phrase "jungle music," the Cotton Club dancers acted out scenes from "old Africa" for the exclusively white clientele, and Ellington quickly became an international star. Duke Ellington deserves his own volume in jazz history. He wrote some of the most profound and lasting big band music each decade until his death in 1974.

Some of Chicago's crop of white musicians, many now resident in the Big Apple, began to feel the pinch as interest waned in the small-group "hot" music that they had borrowed from New Orleans. Young clarinetist Benny Goodman had been taking advantage of his virtuoso technique to ride the post-Wall Street Crash lean years with a series of lucrative studio and pit-band gigs, but his difficult temperament seemed to cut short each engagement.

Once, when reprimanded by a bandleader for joking around during a solo, Goodman replied, "You know how I sound when I'm joking? Well

Above: *Mood Indigo* and *Black and Tan Fantasy* were hits for Duke Ellington's superb big band while it was resident at Harlem's Cotton Club. ●

Right: Benny Goodman's amazing sextet was one of the first top-level racially integrated bands in jazz, and featured star vibraphonist Lionel Hampton and pioneering electric guitarist Charlie Christian. ●

you sound like that all the time." His caustic wit was not designed to make him the most popular man in the music business. Nevertheless, it was Goodman, and his beguiling blend of gutsy riff music, dance arrangements of Tin Pan Alley songs and brilliant, sparkling clarinet, that put big band swing on the mainstream music map.

A tour to the West Coast in 1935 had been uneventful until the very final shows. The Palomar Ballroom in Los Angeles was the scene of a legendary moment in jazz history. Playing a series of arrangements he had only recently bought from Fletcher Henderson, Goodman was met by a packed and ecstatic house, and turned one month's engagement into two. The swing era had begun.

Meanwhile, in the South West, a massive proliferation of talented big band musicians had been taking advantage of a corrupt administration's "lax regime," and enjoying the fruits of a busy nightclub scene. When the Depression bit, fearsome competition for work resulted in a period of frenetic musical development. A host of hard-swinging, individualistic soloists and bands used Kansas City as a jam-session battleground.

Pianist and bandleader Bennie Moten, one of the first wave of black recording artists in 1923, was by 1932 playing a loose, riff-based, blues-drenched music that would become known as "Kansas City swing." When fellow pianist Count Basie stole the best bits of his band four years later, he created one of the most powerful and unforgettable big bands of the period, featuring vital and innovative soloists such as saxophonist Lester Young and trumpeter Buck Clayton.

The New York and Kansas City movement came together in 1938, when promoter John Hammond made the unprecedented move of booking New York's premier classical music venue Carnegie Hall for an all-star jazz night. Benny Goodman and his band were to play a summarized jazz history, performing music by the Original Dixieland Jazz Band, Bix Beiderbecke, Louis Armstrong and others. Realizing that it was impossible to recreate the Ellington sound without the Ellington musicians, they borrowed Johnny Hodges, Harry Carney and Cootie Williams from the Ellington front line. Count Basie, still unknown in New York, appeared in a small group with Young and Clayton.

In 1938, swing was big business. The effect on jazz history was far-reaching. For the first time, jazz musicians were coming to be seen as artists. Fans were starting to understand the processes of improvisation, and even followed their favorite soloists from band to band. Racially integrated groups, although a long way from having a comfortable time, were at last working. And there were proper jazz clubs springing up to cater specifically for a music that had hitherto made its home in speakeasies, ballrooms and movie theaters.

The competitiveness that had characterized the Kansas City scene was making itself felt in New York. Top soloists from the big bands began congregating at a number of sympathetic clubs, where they could jam after-hours, and

...it is 1935, and Benny Goodman plays to an ecstatic house in Los Angeles, turning one month's engagement into two.

41

stretch themselves in a way the big band format rarely allowed them. At Minton's Playhouse, a musician-owned club in Harlem, and Monroe's Uptown House, a popular 52nd Street musicians' haunt, circles were developing within circles.

A young, technically advanced trumpeter known as Dizzy Gillespie and an eccentric, introspective pianist called Thelonious Monk, began collaborating. They complicated standard chord sequences, swapping chords and extending them, in a (usually successful) attempt to throw other musicians off.

Meanwhile, in a swing band run by elegant pianist Teddy Wilson, drummer Kenny Clarke was experimenting with the rhythmic end of the music, moving the beat up onto the cymbals where it would be more fluid, and playing strange, irregular accents on the snare and toms (known, in the vernacular of the day, as "dropping bombs"). Wilson sacked him. He knew a good thing when he heard it, however, and re-hired Clarke as house drummer at Minton's. Assembling a core band, Clarke sought out the modernists, picking up Gillespie and Monk and, on a trip to Monroe's, hiring the man who would be the modernist movement's figurehead and genius.

Charlie "Bird" Parker, nicknamed after his predilection for chicken dishes, was a young alto saxophonist who had been born and raised in the Kansas City jazz hothouse of the 1930s. He had idolized Basie's tenor saxophonist Lester Young, and taught himself to emulate Young's elegantly flowing, fast-fingered swing style.

A self-destructive genius with an intensely instinctive approach to improvisation, Parker would come to represent everything that was both good and bad about the jazz scene. As a

Charlie "Bird" Parker was to become the modernist movement's figurehead and genius.

musician, he set impossibly high standards. Several swing-era saxophonists claim to have lost all ambition on the instrument after having heard Parker at work. The rest of his life, however, was a shambles characterized by drug addiction, depression and debauchery.

Just a few years after Goodman's Carnegie Hall triumph, Charlie Parker and Dizzy Gillespie were bringing about a musical revolution. The frenetic new music, given the onomatopoeic tags "rebop" and then "bebop," would change jazz for all time.

WILLIAM GOTTLIEB

Plenty of older musicians expressed their disapproval at what they saw as a self-indulgent, impenetrable music. Reactionary jazz fans around the world began a revivalist movement that would reverberate for years to come. New Orleans originals such as Armstrong, Bechet and an old trumpet player called Bunk Johnson who claimed (dubiously) to have worked with Buddy Bolden, won an enthusiastic new following. But the action was with the beboppers, and Parker and company began a series of recordings that, to this day, crackle with the excitement and intelligence of artistic revolution in motion.

The bebop period did not last long – the intense

solos and short, fractured tunes were just too unsettling, too feverish to sit comfortably in the jazz mainstream. Charlie Parker burned himself out, and died at the age of 34, in 1955. His style had not been given the opportunity to develop. He just seemed to come and go like a blinding white light, leaving a legacy of stunningly inspired recordings, myths and cult "Bird lives" graffiti.

Before Parker died, he had hired a young, St Louis-born trumpeter called Miles Davis to replace Gillespie in his working band. Davis rarely cut the mustard. Uncomfortable at the kind of super-human tempo Parker enjoyed, his solos, pieced together from his favorite Gillespie phrases, faltered precariously. Inquiring and determined by nature, he sought out his own more relaxed version of the new music. In 1949 Davis collaborated with the gifted arranger Gil Evans and a group of like-minded musicians to record a softly-spoken, mellow version of bebop. *The Birth of the Cool* featured saxophonists Lee Konitz and Gerry Mulligan, and helped launch an entire new school of modern jazz, based around the West Coast. White jazz stars such as Dave Brubeck and Chet Baker would turn this music into something approaching pop during the following decade.

Other musicians injected a little raw rhythm and blues into the bebop language. Out of New York, and northern industrial centers such as Chicago, Detroit and Philadelphia, a tough modern jazz sound known as "hard-bop" developed. Central in the movement was drummer Art Blakey, whose series of Jazz Messengers lineups featured many of the most important young players around. The Jazz Messengers continued to function as a showcase for young musicians, and as a flag-

flyer for hard-bop, up until the time of Art Blakey's death in 1990.

But bebop's legacy was not just musical. Heroin began to figure more prominently than ever before in the jazz lifestyle. Nurtured partly by the pressures of playing a difficult music in the some-times noisy and frustrating environment of the club, and partly by a kind of underground chic, hard drugs became an undeniable feature of the jazz social scene. Some musicians even believed that drugs would help them play like Parker. Over the next few decades, heroin would demand a terrible toll from the jazz scene.

In 1955 Miles Davis, himself recovering from a period severely marred by drug addiction, hired pianist Red Garland, bassist Paul Chambers, drummer Philly Joe Jones and a young Philadelphian tenor saxophonist called John Coltrane. Coltrane had a sound and approach quite unlike anyone else. Davis, only 29 himself, encouraged him, showing the instinctive foresight and judgment that would characterize his dealings with young musicians throughout his career.

As the leader's lines became more introspective, Coltrane developed an obsession with harmony that would force him to unleash torrents of notes in his quest to play every-thing he heard. There was magic in the con-trast, and the partnership recorded some of the finest hard-bop music. By 1958 new doors were opening, and John Coltrane was preparing to play his part in the next jazz revolution.

Left: Masters of bop – trumpeter Fats Navarro with tenor saxophonist Charlie Rouse and pianist/composer Tadd Dameron. ●

Below: Pianist Dave Brubeck led one of the most endearingly popular bands in jazz, recording hits such as *Take Five* and *Unsquare Dance*. ●

BOB WILLOUGHBY

> **The boys dug in with some of the best playing since we left New York. I don't know what it was, but the crowd went wild, and then – boom!**
>
> BENNY GOODMAN

CHUCK STEWART

A BIG SWING

Left: Jimmie Lunceford's big band blended gutsy swing with overt showmanship, and was one of the most popular black bands of the early 1930s. ●

Left inset: Bennie Goodman. ●

Above: Bandleader/singer Cab Calloway was an extrovert, charismatic performer with a taste for the musically (and lyrically) exotic. ●

The 1930s heralded the advent of jazz as the popular music of the day, with big bands jamming the American airwaves and blasting the dance-halls. The variety was impressive. Louis Armstrong used the big band as a background for his own brand of dazzling trumpet and pop vocals. In Kansas City, Bennie Moten and Count Basie created a riff-and-blues style that introduced an array of star soloists, and helped pave the way for both bebop and rock and roll. Competition from Oklahoma-born but Kansas City-based bands, such as Walter Page's Blue Devils and Andy Kirk and his Clouds of Joy, kept KC musicians on the edge, battling it out for swing supremacy.

In the East, Duke Ellington created arrangements of exquisite delicacy and sophistication, writing music for his musicians, rather than hiring musicians to play his music. Meanwhile, Fletcher Henderson and Jimmie Lunceford led powerful but polished, fast-moving swing bands, designed to make maximum impact in the minimum time. It was the swing orchestra of white clarinetist Benny Goodman, however, that put the music on the mainstream map, investing Tin Pan Alley songs with a climactic urgency that set younger audiences tearing up their seats and dancing in the aisles. ▶

Above: Brilliant swing improviser Coleman Hawkins was the father of the tenor saxophone. His big tone and powerful swing set high standards, and made him a hero among saxophonists. ●

Above: A luminous, energetic cornetist, Rex Stewart replaced Louis Armstrong in Fletcher Henderson's band before joining Duke Ellington in 1934. He was a feature of the band for the next 11 years. ●

MICHAEL OCHS ARCHIVES

Above: One of the very few jazz musicians to excel at both saxophone and trumpet, Benny Carter was a major swing-era talent, and wrote immaculate arrangements for Fletcher Henderson, McKinney's Cotton Pickers, Benny Goodman and Chick Webb. ●

MILESTONES:
THE BIG BAND

From the Fletcher Henderson model of the late 1920s to the blasting dance orchestras of the 1940s, the big band would vary in size over the years. But taking as a model the classic swing-era lineup that Count Basie employed for *One O'Clock Jump*, the 1930s big band would be arranged as follows:

Brass: Three trumpets and three trombones formed a powerful six-piece brass chorus. Each section had a soloist or lead player, sometimes two. Trumpeters began to extend the instrument's range, so that they could be heard over the huge orchestras.

Reeds: With so much big band music riff-based, arrangers liked to set the brass and the reeds against each other, playing in a kind of call-and-response formation. Reed players would double on the clarinet and a number of saxophones, but Basie's basic lineup used one alto saxophone, two tenors and a baritone.

Piano: The new swing sound put more emphasis on the solo. Bandleaders such as Basie and Duke Ellington enjoyed peppering their piano solos with contrasting blasts from the powerful wind sections.

Guitar: By the mid-1930s, the banjo had practically died out. Guitarists such as Allen Reuss (with Benny Goodman) and, most famously, Freddie Green (with Basie) made careers out of providing unobtrusive but rock-steady rhythmic accompaniment.

Bass: Now exclusively playing the string bass (rather than the tuba), the bassist provided a *pizzicato* line through the chord sequence.

Drums: Powerful and noisy, big bands demanded demonstrative drummers. A new breed of intense, hard-swinging sticksmen such as Jo Jones, Gene Krupa and Buddy Rich rose to the occasion, mixing their craft with a stylish element of showmanship.

MICHAEL OCHS ARCHIVES

Above: Cab Calloway was an outrageous showman. As he conducted, his great mop of hair would unfold into something as wild as the music his band blew behind him. His hip, slang-infused songs were packed with thinly veiled references to drug culture. ●

MICHAEL OCHS ARCHIVES

Left: The late 1930s orchestra of pianist Count Basie was one of the finest of the swing era, and encapsulated the Kansas City blues-and-riff sound. Basie was an elegant, minimalist soloist, but the band's collective sound was a big, exciting blast. ●

Right: A true genius, Basie's Lester Young sounded unlike any other tenor saxophonist. His pretty, limpid sound and fleet lines would prove to be a big inspiration to Charlie Parker and the beboppers. ●

Below: Hard-swinging trumpeter Buck Clayton was a mainstay of Count Basie's classic band, and would stay at the forefront of the mainstream jazz movement for decades to come. ●

Right: Clark Terry came to prominence as a big band trumpeter in the 1940s, with Basie and Duke Ellington. His mellow and intricate style would be an inspiration to fellow St Louis-born trumpeter Miles Davis. ●

Below: Benny Goodman's exciting orchestra inspired the big band craze, and the clarinetist himself became dubbed "The King of Swing." ●

Below: Initially, Goodman did not want to hire guitarist Charlie Christian, but when he heard this unique proto-bopper he changed his mind. ●

Below: Flash showman but subtle improviser, drummer/vibraphonist Lionel Hampton led his own bands and played in Goodman's superb sextet. ●

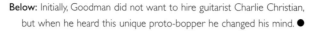

Above: Trombonist Tommy and saxophonist Jimmy Dorsey were distinguished musicians. They argued like true brothers. ●

Above: The rich, nostalgic sound of trombonist Glenn Miller's hit swing dance band has become synonymous with memories of wartime. ●

RAY AVERY'S JAZZ ARCHIVES

Left: Virtuoso clarinetist Artie Shaw rivaled Goodman technically, but not commercially. For a brief period, Billie Holiday was his band vocalist, but the pressures placed on a racially integrated group while on tour proved too great. ●

RAY AVERY'S JAZZ ARCHIVES

Left: Trumpeter Roy Eldridge was the finest swing trumpeter of the 1940s, but suffered hurtful abuse from racist audiences while touring with white bandleaders Gene Krupa and Artie Shaw. ●

MILESTONES:
THE INFLUENCES BEHIND BEBOP

By the late 1930s, with the swing era reaching its zenith, a number of big band musicians had already begun playing music that would inspire Charlie Parker and Dizzy Gillespie to make the final leap of faith into modern jazz.

Lester Young: Soft-toned tenor saxophone genius Lester Young had been mocked when he first joined Count Basie. But his fleet, fast-fingered style and sophisticated, scaler approach made him a hero to the first generation of bebop musicians. Charlie Parker would learn his solos by heart, and a group of saxophonists, including Zoot Sims, Stan Getz and Al Cohn, would play in a Young-influenced style throughout the decades to come.

Charlie Christian: The first great electric guitarist, Christian soloed with an unprecedented sophistication, and was recorded at Minton's Playhouse jamming with the pioneers of bebop. His short but brilliant career was tragically curtailed by tuberculosis at the age of 26.

Art Tatum: This complex, virtuoso pianist was said already to be at the height of his powers in the late 1930s. His speed of execution and his readiness to complicate standard chord sequences are both reflected in Bud Powell's classic bebop compositions.

Roy Eldridge: One of the swing era's truly great trumpeters, Eldridge is often cited as having had an influence on Gillespie. He jammed at Minton's Playhouse, and his stunning command of the extended register and fiery, confident attack certainly contributed to Gillespie's ambitious approach. Roy Eldridge was a master.

Jimmy Blanton: Duke Ellington's bassist was rarely given credit for his role during this period. His clever, harmonically aware approach affected many of New York's bassists, and paved the way for the crucial role played by the bass in the new bebop small group.

Above and Right: The most celebrated big band leader and composer in jazz history, Duke Ellington cut an odd path through the swing era. Against a backdrop of blood-and-guts, riff-and-swing outfits, the best Ellington moments vibrated with a lush, almost exotic musical texture — as urbane and elegant as the Duke himself.

From Harlem's Cotton Club, the Ellington Orchestra soon graduated to the concert hall, and toured tirelessly and internationally, battling from the thick of the big band era to the thin of the bebop period, before bursting back into the forefront of the jazz scene with a history-making appearance at the 1956 Newport Festival. When he died in 1974, Ellington's compositions included huge, extended suites, collections of sacred music, film scores and a host of swing hits. Today, he is commonly regarded as one of the United States' finest-ever composers.

Many of Ellington's musicians devoted almost their entire careers to the band, growing with the music while the music grew with them. The shy but brilliant composer/arranger Billy Strayhorn *(pictured opposite with Ellington)* worked with the Duke for 28 years (1939-67), and contributed some of the band's finest moments. But it was their charismatic leader and stylish pianist who held the band together, inspiring the very best from his musicians, and leaving the richest legacy in jazz. Indispensable Ellington recordings include: *Black and Tan Fantasy* and *Mood Indigo* from the Cotton Club period; his triumphant 1956 *At Newport;* and the 1962 *Money Jungle* trio album, showcasing what a fine pianist Duke Ellington was. ●

Right: Art Tatum was a genius. He had an elaborate, challenging harmonic approach, and the fastest fingers in jazz. ●

Far right: The creator of a lush, romantic sound on the tenor saxophone, Ben Webster was one of Duke Ellington's star soloists in the early 1940s, and remained a popular, busy musician until his death in 1973. ●

Right: Django Reinhardt and Stéphane Grappelli were the first musicians to develop a jazz style based on a European musical heritage, rather than a borrowed African-American one. Guitarist Reinhardt *(pictured with his foot on a chair)*, a Belgian gypsy, was born in a caravan, surrounded by all the flamboyant musical tradition that entailed. Despite losing two of his fretting fingers in a caravan fire, he developed a stunningly intricate, rococo guitar style. French violinist Stéphane Grappelli met him in the mid-1930s, and together they formed the Quintette du Hot Club de France: the fearsomely swinging string-based outfit pictured, and one of the most prolifically recorded groups of the swing era. ●

Below: Ella Fitzgerald joined the orchestra of drummer Chick Webb *(pictured)* in the mid-1930s. Soon her light and attractive vocal style became one of the best-loved sounds in jazz. ●

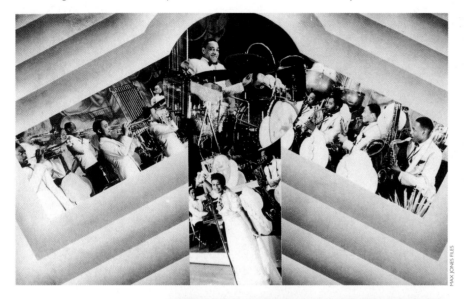

MAX JONES FILES

MILESTONES:
STRIDE AND BOOGIE-WOOGIE PIANO HEROES

During the late 1930s and early 1940s, the art of solo piano was reaching a new peak of artistry. Stride pianists battled it out among themselves, competing at a sophisticated, ragtime-based music. Meanwhile, boogie-woogie, a tough, jazz-blues hybrid that had been around since the 1920s, enjoyed a sudden boom in popularity.

Art Tatum: Tatum was perhaps the greatest virtuoso in the history of jazz piano. His music went beyond stride, contributing to the development of modern jazz.

Fats Waller: Waller was a key figure in the stride movement. His confident left-hand accompaniment and surprisingly delicate, nimble way with the fat fingers of his right hand, marked a great musician, whose show-biz approach could never cloud his artistry.

Right: Nicknamed "Lady Day" by saxophonist and close friend Lester Young (whom she named "Prez"), Billie Holiday spent her life fighting to retain dignity in undignified surroundings, struggling against drug addiction and racism. Her music often reflected a tough life, but some of her best earlier recordings bounce along with a surprising, refreshing joy. ●

RAY AVERY'S JAZZ ARCHIVES

James P. Johnson: If it was Waller who brought stride to the attention of the public, it was Johnson who brought it to the attention of Waller. Possibly the greatest pure stride pianist of them all, Johnson taught Waller, dabbled in classical composition, and influenced virtually every pianist from the mid-1930s onward.

Willie "The Lion" Smith: Greatly admired by Duke Ellington, as well as immediate rivals such as Waller and Johnson, Smith began his career as a ragtime pianist and was one of the Harlem stride originals.

Right: Woody Herman *(standing)* was a big band leader who incorporated bebop into his music. ●

Far right: When singer and trumpeter Billy Eckstine assembled his big band in the 1940s, he hired many leading modernists, including Parker and Gillespie. ●

MAX JONES FILES

DUNCAN P. SCHIEDT

Meade Lux Lewis: Possibly the most popular figure in the boogie-woogie craze, Lewis began recording in the 1920s. He collaborated in the 1930s with pianists Pete Johnson and Albert Ammons in what was billed as "The Boogie-Woogie Trio."

Jimmy Yancey: Yancey's rocking and bluesy style, while less sophisticated than that of his rivals, was rarely matched for swing and drive.

❝ *Holy the groaning saxophone! Holy the bop apocalypse! Holy the jazzbands marijuana hipsters peace peyote pipes & drums!* ❞

ALLEN GINSBERG FROM *FOOTNOTE TO HOWL*

BEBOP: 52ND STREET ICONS

THREE DEUCES *Presents* CHARLIE PARKER AND HIS BAND *featuring* [...] DAVIS TRUMPET MAX ROACH DRUMS DUKE JORDAN PIANO TOMMY POTTER

WILLIAM GOTTLIEB

I n the 1940s, Manhattan's 52nd Street was the scene of a musical revolution. The swing era had created a number of charismatic and original improvisers: men such as the fleet and romantic, porkpie-hatted Lester Young, and the energetic, sophisticated guitarist Charlie Christian. Under their influence the youngest generation of black jazz musicians grew bored with the unwieldy big band format, and disillusioned with what they saw as black music turned into a white industry.

Informal jam sessions at sympathetic clubs worked like underground jazz laboratories, until a new music was born – magnificent and fully formed – and displayed in 52nd Street jazz clubs such as the Onyx, the Three Deuces and the Spotlight. First called "rebop," and then "bebop," the new music took the chord sequences of standard songs, complicated them, and added new, fractured melodies. And bebop's top practitioners, Charlie Parker and Dizzy Gillespie, soloed with a fierce, disorienting virtuosity. Not everybody loved it, but there was no going back. From now on, "Bird and Diz" were the new Bechet and Armstrong, and young jazz musicians, with their goatee beards and berets, would have to work hard to emulate their idols.

Left: Dexter Gordon's dynamic mixture of swing and bebop was packaged with one of the biggest tenor sax tones in the business. ●

Above: Clubs such as the Three Deuces were bebop's first home, and turned New York's 52nd Street into a mecca for the new music. ●

CHUCK STEWART

Far left and Left: Pianist Thelonious Sphere Monk was there at the very beginning of the bebop revolution, joining drummer Kenny Clarke and trumpeter Dizzy Gillespie in the legendary jam sessions at Monroe's Uptown House and Mintons. His style did not, however, fit into the bebop mould in the same way as that of his contemporary, Bud Powell. Monk's music was deeply personal: an offbeat, often wryly humorous collection of brittle, cleverly structured tunes and oddly timed and dissonant solos. He worked with many of the greats of the hard-bop era (including, notably, John Coltrane), and led a long-running quartet with saxophonist Charlie Rouse. Some of his best recorded work came at the beginning of his career, and can be heard on two volumes on the Blue Note label, entitled *Genius of Modern Music*. ●

MICHAEL OCHS ARCHIVES

WILLIAM GOTTLIEB

Left: One of the architects of modern jazz, Kenny Clarke pioneered a subtle and fluid approach to jazz drumming. He has influenced every drummer since. ●

MILESTONES:
BEBOP —
THE INSTRUMENTS

Bebop made new demands on jazz instrumentalists. The complex and fractured tunes were difficult to play, and the chord sequences tricky to improvise through.

Brass: Trumpeters such as Dizzy Gillespie and Fats Navarro pushed the instrument to its limits, extending its range and playing at a fearsome speed. The slide trombone, favored in early jazz for its thick *glissandos*, was not ideally suited to the fast-moving and precise new music. But trombonist J.J. Johnson managed to overcome some of the instrument's inherent challenges, and appeared on many of bebop's most important sessions.

Reeds: The clarinet was finally superseded by the saxophone as the foremost reed instrument of jazz. Alto player Charlie Parker had a profound effect on a new generation of saxophonists, who would play faster, and with a less pronounced *vibrato* than before.

Piano: Influenced by Thelonious Monk and Bud Powell, the modern pianists broke their playing up, and developed the art of "comping" — accompanying the lead instruments with deftly timed, attentively voiced chords.

Guitar: Although (with amplification) better able to compete as a lead instrument, the guitar was something of a rarity in the bebop group.

Bass: Bassists such as Charles Mingus and Tommy Potter played a constant 4/4 *pizzicato* line, linking the roots of the chord sequence. With superior amplification and recording facilities, bass solos became a regular feature for the first time.

Drums: Kenny Clarke brought about a revolution in jazz drumming by moving the beat onto the cymbals, and using the snare, toms and bass drum to create an irregular commentary of accents.

WILLIAM GOTTLIEB

This page: Charlie "Bird" Parker was bebop's wayward genius. As a young Kansas City teenager, he had spent the 1930s drifting around the thriving local club scene, enthralled by the sounds of the Basie band, and Lester Young in particular. By the mid-1940s, he had developed a high-speed, harmonically daring style of improvisation that only the brave dared attempt to emulate. But his gargantuan appetites (for food, sex, alcohol and heroin, and often more than one at the same time) made carnage of his private life, resulting in breakdowns, breakups and attempted suicide. Charlie Parker is reputed to have once held up his arms to show the needle tracks. "This is my Cadillac," he said. "And this is my house." When Parker died in 1955 at the age of 35, a doctor estimated his age from his appearance to be between 50 and 60. Soon, "Bird lives" graffiti began to appear around New York.

One of the most charismatic jazz improvisers, Parker stuns the listener with his grace, beauty and virtuosity. Essential recordings include the large collection made for Dial, and the *Live at Storyville* album released by Blue Note. ●

DUNCAN P. SCHIEDT

MICHAEL OCHS ARCHIVES

Above: Bud Powell was an intense, inspired bebop pianist. His career, however, was blighted by mental health problems. ●

Above: Max Roach was the regular drummer in Charlie Parker's classic late 1940s quintet, and led some of the most powerful political statements of the 1960s. ●

Below: Trumpeter Miles Davis was still a teenager when he joined Charlie Parker's bebop quintet. ●

61

DUNCAN P. SCHIEDT

WILLIAM GOTTLIEB

Top left and Right:
Trumpeter Dizzy Gillespie fell so naturally into the role of musical sparring partner for Charlie Parker that very soon the phrase "Bird and Diz" began to trip off the tongue. He was an equally revolutionary force on the jazz scene, and together they made some classic, breathtaking records (including the live and historic *Jazz at Massey Hall*). But their collaboration was relatively short-lived, as Gillespie became frustrated with Parker's unreliability, and Parker resentful of Gillespie's commercial success. The trumpeter went on to spread bebop into the realms of the big band, and showed a deep love for Cuban music, playing a catchy form of Latin jazz.

He is seen *(to the right)*, in the heyday of the bebop movement. The later photograph *(above left)* shows him with fellow trumpet star Miles Davis. Note the curved trumpet bell, a feature that he found allowed him to hear what he was playing more clearly. ●

Right: Powerful, brassy bebop trumpeter Fats Navarro made great music with Parker and Powell, but died tragically in 1950 from tuberculosis. ●

WILLIAM GOTTLIEB

MICHAEL OCHS ARCHIVES

MILESTONES:

SONNY ROLLINS
IN INTERVIEW

"*At one time I'd get annoyed by people trying to copy me because I thought they should be shooting higher. That was my attitude for quite a while. I can remember sending one guy who wanted to study with me to Coltrane. I thought it would be better for him because I was too much of an erratic player. Now I feel flattered and good about it, because it helps me feel like I've contributed something. As one gets older one's legacy looms more in one's mind. I've borrowed from Ben Webster, Don Byas, Lester Young – all of these guys that have helped me – so it makes me feel more worthy if some of the young guys get something from me.*

My music fulfills a physical and a spiritual part of my life. If I'm not feeling well, if I play my saxophone it makes me feel physically better. Or if I'm on the road, and I'm not able to play for a couple of days something feels really wrong. Then, when I play, everything's alright again. I don't know what I'd do without it.

There are dangers involved in being a person who just improvises. Sometimes things still don't come out as I'd want. They're different each time and I'm trying to pull them out the air, but that's the nature of the beast. I'm glad that I'm a person that approaches music that way. To me that's the essence of jazz."

MICHAEL OCHS ARCHIVES

Above: Tadd Dameron played piano with Kenny Clarke, Fats Navarro and Miles Davis, but he is best remembered as one of bebop's finest composers. ●

WILLIAM GOTTLIEB

Above: When trumpeter Red Rodney toured the Southern States with Charlie Parker, he was billed as "Albino Red," in an eccentric attempt to avoid the problems faced by racially mixed bands. ●

DUNCAN P. SCHIEDT

Above: Erroll Garner, with his thumping left hand and syncopated right, was not a bebop pianist; but he was an immensely popular artist during the bebop period, and recorded with Charlie Parker. ●

Above: The fabulous Sonny Stitt materialized around the same time as Parker, playing in a remarkably similar style. He graduated to the tenor saxophone, in order to distinguish himself from Bird. ●

Above: Vibraphone player Milt Jackson (nicknamed "Bags") is one of the purest improvisers in the bebop style. He recorded brilliantly with Monk, before joining the legendary Modern Jazz Quartet (MJQ). ●

Above: Dexter Gordon (*pictured right*) played even better than he dressed, bridging the gap between swing and bop with the lushest ballads and the strongest blues. In the 1980s, he began a second career as a film actor. ●

66 *I loved working with Gil because he was so meticulous and creative, and I trusted his musical arrangements completely... Gil and I were something special together musically.* 99

MILES DAVIS

BOB BAKER

EAST COAST HARD-BOP
& WEST COAST COOL

Bebop had set a pace that was never going to be sustained. The next challenge was to create a music that did not step back from the advances made by Parker, Gillespie and company, but was capable of expressing a greater range of emotion.

Hard-bop spoke the same language, but took a few liberties with the grammar and syntax. It was a plainer, more humane music, and it left space for virtually endless variation, borrowing from Latin, African and classical sources. By embracing gospel music and rhythm and blues, it paved the way for what, in decades to come, would be called funk.

Meanwhile, on the West Coast, a group of predominantly white musicians, playing Hollywood soundtracks by day and jazz by night, began to reflect their more laid-back and sunny environment, with a lightly-swinging brand of modern jazz. Trumpeter and vocalist Chet Baker turned insipid ballads into vehicles for painfully touching performances; and pianist Dave Brubeck, touring with brilliant saxophonist Paul Desmond, caught the American imagination with a series of catchy tunes and hit records.

Left: The hard-bop era saw trumpeter Miles Davis grow into a lyrical and laid-back master improviser. ●

Above: Horace Silver, hard-bop piano master. ●

GAI TERRELL

67

CHUCK STEWART

MICHAEL OCHS ARCHIVES

Left: Horace Silver's funky, rumbling, Gospel-influenced piano style was an exciting feature of many early Blue Note label classics. ●

Above: Jimmy Smith turned the bubbly tones of the Hammond B3 organ into the most soulful sound in jazz. ●

Below: Alto saxophonist Jackie McLean gave Parker's bebop style a tough and acerbic edge. ●

RAY AVERY'S JAZZ ARCHIVES

MICHAEL OCHS ARCHIVES

Above: Freddie Hubbard was only 20 in 1958, but he was already an exciting, original improviser with roots in Clifford Brown's brassy bop style. In the 1960s and 1970s he would experiment with free jazz and fusion, but he never forgot his hard-bop roots. ●

MODERN JAZZ TRUMPET

FAMILY TREE

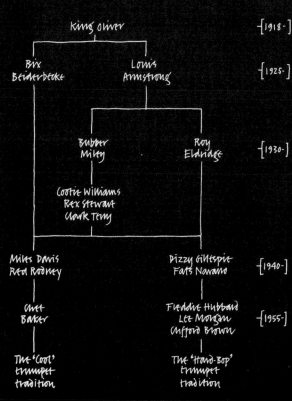

King Oliver — [1918-]

Bix Beiderbecke — [1925-]

Louis Armstrong

Bubber Miley — [1930-]

Roy Eldridge

Cootie Williams
Rex Stewart
Clark Terry

Miles Davis
Red Rodney — [1940-]

Dizzy Gillespie
Fats Navarro

Chet Baker — [1955-]

Freddie Hubbard
Lee Morgan
Clifford Brown

The 'cool' trumpet tradition

The 'Hard-Bop' trumpet tradition

Louis Armstrong's brassy blast lay behind bluesy swing trumpeters Miley and Williams and fiery virtuoso Eldridge. In the 1940s and 1950s, Gillespie combined both styles. Bix Beiderbecke's lyrical approach and Terry's fleet elegance contributed to Miles Davis' "cool" school, ultimately encapsulated by Chet Baker's West Coast style.

69

CHUCK STEWART

Above: Trumpeter Clifford Brown's mid-1950s band with drummer Max Roach was one of the highlights of hard-bop, but it was short-lived. Brown died tragically in a road accident in 1956. ●

DAVID REDFERN

Left: Lee Morgan's snarling, aggressive trumpet style was a cornerstone of one of the Jazz Messengers' finest units. Later, he had a huge soul-jazz hit called *The Sidewinder*. ●

Below: One of the alto saxophonists who picked up where Charlie Parker left off, Lou Donaldson was an immaculate bopper and a soulful blues player. ●

MICHAEL OCHS ARCHIVES

Above: Tenor saxophonist Sonny Rollins found his voice among the hard-bop generation. His 1956 *Saxophone Colossus* is a modern jazz masterpiece; but in the decades to come he would loosen up his style into a unique mixture of bop, calypso and free jazz. A titanic tenor force, he remains one of the most important musicians ever to pick up the instrument. ●

MICHAEL OCHS ARCHIVES

RAY AVERY'S JAZZ ARCHIVES

DAVID REDFERN

This page and Right: Over four decades, the intense, thunderous sound of Art Blakey behind the kit was synonymous with hard-bop. He co-led the original Jazz Messengers with pianist Horace Silver, and retained the title when Silver left to form his own groups, continuing to people the band with the very best up-and-coming instrumentalists the music had to offer (*see right*).

The crisp Blakey sound arose from a combination of fearsome energy and swing, and the drummer's ability to play in more than one signature at once - something which other drummers, including Max Roach and Elvin Jones, could also do, but which no-one else made sound so lucid and logical.

Sadly, Blakey died in 1990, and jazz lost another giant. Thankfully, he recorded prodigiously. Recommended albums include the two-volume 1954 *A Night at Birdland*, and the 1960 *A Night in Tunisia*, both available on Blue Note. ●

JAZZ MESSENGERS

FAMILY TREE.

ART BLAKEY
1ST GENERATION

| Clifford Brown (tr) | Lou Donaldson (as) | Kenny Dorham (tr) | Horace Silver (p) | Hank Mobley (ts) | Jackie McLean (as) |

2ND GENERATION

| Lee Morgan (tr) | Johnny Griffin (ts) | Benny Golson (ts) | Bobby Timmons (p) |

'60s

| Freddie Hubbard (tr) | Wayne Shorter (ts) | Cedar Walton (p) | Woody Shaw (tr) |

LEAN '70s
|
Bobby Watson
(as)

PROLIFIC '80s

| Wynton Marsalis (tr) | Terence Blanchard (tr) | Wallace Roney (tr) | Mulgrew Miller (p) | Benny Green (p) | Kenny Garrett (as) |

as-alto saxophone   ts-tenor saxophone   tr-trumpet   p-piano

From the first Jazz Messengers of the 1950s, to the group of young instrumentalists gathered around him in his final years, Art Blakey's bands were the eye of the hard-bop hurricane.

Above and Right: In the 1950s, Miles Davis blossomed into a jazz genius. His hard-bop sextet featured bluesy alto saxophonist Cannonball Adderley, controversial tenor saxophonist John Coltrane, subtle pianist Bill Evans, top bassist Paul Chambers and immaculate drummer Jimmy Cobb. He also collaborated on a series of orchestral masterpieces with arranger Gil Evans (*right*), blowing exquisite trumpet on *Sketches of Spain*, *Miles Ahead* and *Porgy and Bess*. ●

Clockwise from top left: The Modern Jazz Quartet played quiet hard-bop. Their popular "chamber jazz" was presented like classical music. ●

Gentle, romantic and impressionistic, Bill Evans' piano style was unique. ●

Lennie Tristano was a gifted pianist but a demanding taskmaster, and one of the leading theorists of jazz. ●

Gerry Mulligan's hard-swinging West Coast baritone saxophone was one of the most popular sounds in jazz. ●

Lee Konitz and Warne Marsh were students of "Cool School" theorist Tristano, and are pictured performing with him here. ●

Left: Trumpeter, singer and icon: Chet Baker's mixture of charismatic, laid-back musical style and playboy good looks made him one of the most photographed musicians in jazz. He played and sang with a cool, melodic directness, but spent his career battling with heroin addiction. ●

Above: Paul Desmond, brilliant alto saxophonist, played in Dave Brubeck's famous quartet. ●

Above: West Coast bad boy Art Pepper was an inspired alto saxophonist, but led an unpredictable, drug-fuelled lifestyle. ●

BOB WILLOUGHBY

Above: Dave Brubeck remains one of the most popular and widely known figures in modern jazz. His most famous quartet, with alto saxophonist Paul Desmond, played a softly swinging music and specialized in odd but catchy tunes, such as *Take Five* and *Unsquare Dance*. ●

MILESTONES:

DAVE BRUBECK
IN INTERVIEW

"For years people have thought that I was a classical musician who turned to jazz. But it's actually the exact opposite. I was a jazz musician, and then I went to study with Milhaud. He told me never to give up jazz, if I wanted to express my culture. If you're from the United States you had to accept the jazz idiom. He'd say the two best US composers are Gershwin and Ellington, and then he'd say that the ones that were going to survive would be the ones that have used the jazz idiom, such as Charles Ives and Bernstein and Copland.

At college I had a big band. When I was in the army I had a big band. So I went through that when I was very young. I preferred something the size of the octet, that was an interesting group. I had a trio after that, and then the quartet. You get to play more with a smaller group.

It was the trio that made the breakthrough. We became the new combo of the year in Downbeat *and* Metronome *in '49. We started playing all the colleges on the West Coast. We'd play for nothing, or whatever they could afford to pay.*

We reached about the widest audience of everybody. The same night that we were playing Carnegie Hall with the New York Philharmonic we had to get into a cab to rush across town to the Basin Street nightclub. So even on the same night we were touching two different audiences."

1958 TODAY THE FREEDOM FACTOR

DANY GIGNOUX

The faster you run, the more likely you are to bump into things.
By 1958, jazz had set itself a furious pace, and ambitious musicians were
already becoming dissatisfied with what sounded like the limits to hard-bop.
Too many improvisers were playing the same old scales over the same
old chord sequences, but just doing it faster and more aggressively. ▶

Right: Bass clarinet virtuoso Eric Dolphy. ●
Above: The graphic Art Ensemble of Chicago. ●

CAPITAL RECORDS INC

Trumpeter Miles Davis, a painfully cool, sharply dressed cult hero, was by now a leading figure in the modern jazz scene. He began to build upon the spacious, sparse and simpler sound of his 1950s band. Scrapping the chord sequences, which were inhibiting the soloists and forcing them merely to scramble from one tonality to the next, he began replacing them with particular scales known as "modes." This allowed the musician considerable time to think and improvise melodically over an attractive, floating, harmonically static wash.

Kind of Blue, recorded in 1959 and showcasing the new sound, was a masterpiece, and is still commonly considered the finest album in jazz history. Over five startlingly simple tunes, Davis sets up a dramatic contrast between his own perfectly sculptured, almost Zen-like improvisations, and the complex, disturbing tumult of notes from his partner John Coltrane on tenor saxophone. Decades later, it sounds as fresh and immediate as anything recorded since.

By 1959, new and more radical changes were taking place elsewhere on the jazz scene. A young, independently minded saxophonist from Texas, called Ornette Coleman, had spent the last decade and a half touring with rhythm and blues bands, and practicing an approach to modern jazz so offbeat that he can remember being paid not to play. Stranded in New Orleans in 1949, after his latest musical transgression had got him beaten up, his saxophone thrown from the top of a hill, he met local drummer Ed Blackwell. This began a collaboration that ten years later would turn the jazz world on its head. Settling in Los Angeles in 1953, he began practicing with the other like-minded musicians who would form his classic "free jazz"

quartet of the early 1960s. Ornette Coleman was not simply replacing chords with scales, he was banishing predetermined harmony altogether.

The quartet even looked odd. Coleman and trumpeter Don Cherry grew long beards and shuffled awkwardly, Cherry played a tiny "pocket" trumpet, and Coleman a white plastic alto. Their music was an unpredictable but blues-inflected wail – at once puzzling and yet familiar. When, in November 1959, they booked into the Five Spot Café in New York, their planned two-week engagement turned into two and a half months. But not everyone was impressed. Many musicians either could not, or would not, get their ears around the sound. Dizzy Gillespie remarked, "I don't know what it is, but it's not jazz." Miles Davis reacted bitterly, especially when Coleman began experimenting with the trumpet.

The Ornette Coleman Quartet had shown that music could ignore harmony, or invent its own as it goes along, and still function beautifully as a joyous, integrated experience. There was no going back. The other leading jazz musicians of the day began to flirt with freedom. Gifted modernists such as saxophonists Joe Henderson and Eric Dolphy, trumpeter Freddie Hubbard and pianist Andrew Hill found musical gold in the area between Davis' modal jazz and Coleman's freedom, playing a sometimes wild and daring music that became known as "post-bop." Spiky, unpredictable bassist Charles Mingus used the new freedom to add an assertive, fiery streak to his own blues-drenched music. Even Miles Davis, continuing to surround himself with younger sidemen, responded with a brand of measured freedom, encouraged by a very open-minded band, now featuring Coltrane-influenced saxo-

Above: Blue Note records, with its star-studded musical personnel, became one of the leading sources of the best post-bop jazz. Saxophonist Wayne Shorter recorded a series of dazzling albums for Blue Note. ●

Right: Albert Ayler's big, throaty roar: the controversial sound of the 1960s avant-garde. ●

phonist Wayne Shorter, pianist Herbie Hancock, bassist Ron Carter and drummer Tony Williams.

Musical changes mirrored political changes. The US army had been accompanying black students into previously segregated high schools, and the country was already getting caught up in the explosive civil rights movement when Ornette Coleman's new music enjoyed its first big splash of media coverage. The very word "free" trembled with connotations, but commentators reacted to the music in different ways. Some saw it as a whitening of jazz, as the classical avant-garde was beginning to flirt with similar sounds and theories. To others, it was an expression of social freedom, a statement of the blackness of jazz, returning the music to its rhythmic, rather than harmonic, African roots. Several improvisers began actively to politicize their music.

When John Coltrane left Davis at the beginning of the 1960s, he formed what was to become one of the most celebrated quartets in jazz history, powered thunderously by complex, African-influenced drummer Elvin Jones, whose explosive, battering, polyrhythmic style has been likened to the sound of combat on a war movie soundtrack. Coltrane had a super-intense approach to the saxophone, and hovered on the brink of freedom. He was a deeply religious man, and seemed to hear his music somewhat differently to those around him. The violence in some of Coltrane's playing was a means to an end – a constant journey and struggle toward some kind of spiritual redemption. But it captivated other experimental musicians, who heard in it the expression of the black liberation movement.

Saxophonists Archie Shepp and Albert Ayler drew inspiration from the sound. Ayler took it to its extremes, eschewing even the standard tone of a saxophone, and blowing strained and scary blasts that combined a folky simplicity with challenging, frightening power. Keyboard player and big band leader Sun Ra extended his unique "myth" approach to his own extraordinary big band music. He politicized it with a complex, extended metaphor that involved his claiming that he had been sent to Earth from Saturn, and dressing his musicians up as spacemen.

As the underground art scene of the 1960s continued to develop, jazz musicians adopted a kind of self-help approach to the avant-garde, organizing their own concerts in unorthodox venues, such as libraries, bookshops, small theaters and even each other's loft apartments. In Chicago, pianist and composer Muhal Richard Abrams got together with two associates to found a nonprofit organization dedicated to furthering the new music. They called it the Association for the Advancement of Creative Music (AACM). Generations of important jazz musicians would graduate from this cooperative, and almost immediately it spawned the brilliant Art Ensemble of Chicago and Anthony Braxton's revolutionary trio.

Europe, traditionally a receptive destination for American jazz musicians, was already reacting to the jazz revolution taking place across the Atlantic, with its own avant-garde scene. Musicians from Holland's Instant Composers' Pool

Saxophonists such as Archie Shepp and Albert Ayler drew inspiration from the sound. Ayler took it to its extremes...

DAVID REDFERN

and Germany's Globe Unity Orchestra represented an explosion of talent. In Britain, a group of improvisers, including guitarist Derek Bailey and drummer John Stevens, were experimenting with an even more radically "free" approach.

> The new music was named "fusion" for its fusion of jazz and rock.

However, not all musicians felt like turning their backs on the mainstream. The problem was that in America, by the end of the 1960s, there was not much of a jazz mainstream left. Rock music had completely displaced jazz in economic terms. Jazz gigs were few and far between and record labels were reluctant to invest in an increasingly unpopular music when rock offered easy returns. Miles Davis had already experimented with electric instruments and rock rhythms on his 1968 album *Miles in the Sky*, but more drastic measures were needed now.

Bitches Brew, recorded the following year, was both an almighty hit and a brilliant, uncompromising record. Leading an extended band, with electric keyboards, bass clarinet and percussion, Davis launched a new sound, combining an

DAVID REDFERN

intricate, rock-based modal background with improvised trumpet and saxophone. It was not a bland mix. In fact the record contained some of the most challenging music Davis had ever made, and his groups would sound increasingly savage and ferocious as the 1960s turned into the 1970s. In 1975, blowing odd, electronically distorted lines against a fractured thrash background, the trumpeter felt he had gone as far as he could, and announced his retirement from the business.

The new music, named "fusion" after its fusion of jazz and rock, became dominated by ex-Miles

Davis sidemen. Keyboard player Herbie Hancock dabbled with disco, recording what would be the best-selling jazz record of all time, *Headhunters*. Wayne Shorter recorded his own album, *Super Nova*, within two weeks of playing on *Bitches Brew*, and joined up with keyboard player Joe Zawinul to form the immensely popular fusion band called Weather Report. Other fusion heavyweights, including Chick Corea, Airto Moreira, Jack DeJohnette, Tony Williams and John McLaughlin, all came to the music through Miles Davis.

Albert Ayler had looked to his own African-American folk tradition to help him abandon some of the "rules" defining jazz. In Europe, an equivalent movement began taking shape. North European musicians, such as Coltrane-influenced saxophonist Jan Garbarek and Finnish drummer Edward Vesala, began reproducing the chilly, atmospheric sound of Scandinavian folk within the format of the jazz band. This European approach was less swing-oriented, and was spacier and more textural.

Coincidentally, across the Atlantic a group of American musicians, influenced by pianist Bill Evans, was specializing in a gently persuasive form of fusion, combining jazz improvisation with the aesthetics of romanticism. The room for collaboration was clear. Guitarist Pat Metheny and vibraphone player Gary Burton both recorded for the burgeoning independent European ECM label. Pianist Keith Jarrett abandoned his Ornette Coleman-influenced American quartet to form a European band of sharply un-American sensibilities, with saxophonist Garbarek, bassist Palle Danielsson and drummer Jon Christensen. In 1975 he played his legendary Köln Concert in

West Germany, an inspired solo piano date which became ECM's best-selling record.

At the beginning of the 1980s, the international jazz scene unexpectedly turned its attention back to New Orleans, the city in which it was born. A 19-year-old black trumpet player called Wynton Marsalis, from one of New Orleans' most musical families, was picked up by hard-bop legend Art Blakey, and won a huge following for his extraordinary virtuosity and cheeky charisma. Equally respected in the classical arena, he became the first musician to win Grammy Awards for jazz and classical records in the same year, and the publicity that followed helped revitalize an interest in jazz. The larger record companies began to seek out their own "Wyntons," signing up younger musicians, and established labels such as Blue Note launched big reissue campaigns. Original hard-boppers such as Blakey, Dexter Gordon and Horace Silver saw their careers rejuvenated.

Reasons for the renewed interest in the music were complicated. A dissatisfaction with pop, which was being aimed at increasingly younger markets, probably contributed. Wynton Marsalis – to many, the embodiment and acceptable face of jazz, with his New Orleans heritage, classical training and smart presentation – was certainly important. But not everyone saw Marsalis as a positive influence. He attacked the avant-garde, he attacked fusion and he attacked any form of jazz that did not fit his own vision.

DAVID REDFERN

Important figures, including the great Miles Davis who was enjoying a mid-1980s comeback, publicly criticized Marsalis for making capital out of the music they had pioneered in the 1960s, while at the same time making it harder for them to continue to develop. When Marsalis began to look further back, specializing in a Duke Ellington-influenced swing style, many began to worry about the ability of jazz to reinvent itself, and they feared that it was indeed becoming the museum or period piece that Wynton Marsalis seemed to be advocating.

But jazz development did not stop. Influenced by hiphop's vital and politically aware culture, a group of musicians under the informal leadership of alto saxophonist Steve Coleman began playing a new sound they called "M-Base." Fusion musicians such as saxophonist Michael Brecker and pianist Chick Corea spent the 1980s pushing the limits of their virtuosity into the reaches of the superhuman, and now play contemporary jazz with a seasoned creativity and depth.

In almost every city, one can hear musicians recreating the sounds of New Orleans in the 1920s or New York in the 1930s. Tunes penned by Charlie Parker and Dizzy Gillespie are now known as standards, and saxophonists all over the world study the music of John Coltrane and pray to be blessed with a fraction of his ability. If one knows where to look, one can even catch the latest generation of improvisers and insurgents, making unorthodox free music from household debris.

Above: Outspoken traditionalist Wynton Marsalis, bearing the name of his trumpet idol on his chest. ●

Left: The fast-fingered, electric sound of fusion, courtesy of guitarist Pat Metheny. ●

To me he was like an angel on earth. He struck me that deeply.

ELVIN JONES, ABOUT JOHN COLTRANE

POST-BOP: KIND OF BLUE TO KIND OF FREE

DAVID REDFERN

Left and Above:
John Coltrane *(left)* formed his legendary quartet in 1961. Inspired by the saxophonist's spiritual convictions, and underpinned by the thunderous drumming style of Elvin Jones *(right)*, the band played a turbulent, restless and exhausting music. ●

Miles Davis' 1959 masterpiece *Kind of Blue* opened new doors. Modal jazz – liberating, but less bewildering than the anarchy of total freedom – allowed jazz's hard-bop generation to replace some of the stolid certainties of the traditional chord sequence with the more enigmatic possibilities of scales.

The explosion of activity that followed has become loosely known as "post-bop," but was actually an eclectic mix of approaches. Art Blakey's Jazz Messengers began playing simpler but more distinctive, hard-driven compositions, written by its young band members. John Coltrane attacked the new freedom with a vengeance, filling the space as fast as he could with an approach that would become known as "sheets of sound." The Blue Note label became the home of a roster of brilliant jazz improvisers, including saxophonists Joe Henderson and Wayne Shorter, vibraphone player Bobby Hutcherson, and pianist Andrew Hill, and would produce many of the finest records of the post-bop era.

This page and Right: Miles Davis' 1959 album *Kind of Blue* had been a phenomenal success. After John Coltrane left to form his own band, the trumpeter felt the need to surround himself with younger jazz talent – musicians who would reflect some of the changes wrought by Ornette Coleman. Saxophonist Wayne Shorter, pianist Herbie Hancock, bassist Ron Carter and drummer Tony Williams had much less experience than Davis (in fact the prodigious Williams was only 18 when he joined the band, and was told to grow a moustache in case he was refused entry to some of the jazz clubs) but their exuberance and open-mindedness inspired the trumpeter to play some of the finest music of his career.

The quintet toyed with freedom. The rhythm section would play games with Davis – dropping out, or switching tempo abruptly – and it kept the trumpeter on his toes. Records like the 1966 *Miles Smiles* and the 1968 *Miles in the Sky* still sound fresh and daring today. ●

DAVID REDFERN

MILES DAVIS

F A M I L Y   T R E E

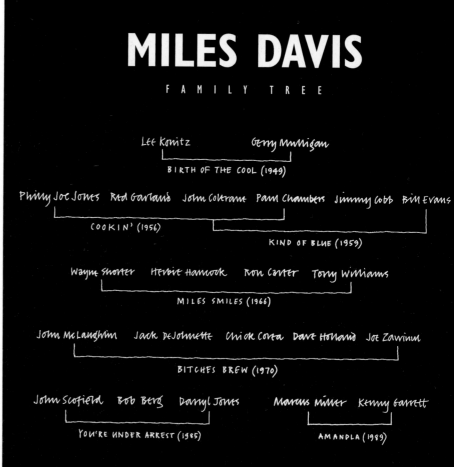

Lee Konitz   Gerry Mulligan
BIRTH OF THE COOL (1949)

Philly Joe Jones   Red Garland   John Coltrane   Paul Chambers   Jimmy Cobb   Bill Evans
COOKIN' (1956)
KIND OF BLUE (1959)

Wayne Shorter   Herbie Hancock   Ron Carter   Tony Williams
MILES SMILES (1966)

John McLaughlin   Jack DeJohnette   Chick Corea   Dave Holland   Joe Zawinul
BITCHES BREW (1970)

John Scofield   Bob Berg   Darryl Jones   Marcus Miller   Kenny Garrett
YOU'RE UNDER ARREST (1985)   AMANDLA (1989)

Miles Davis' 1960s quintet was a perfect example of the trumpeter's uncanny ability to find the right musicians for the job. His different bands were almost like training grounds for the latest jazz developments. As the trumpeter pushed forward he introduced some of the most significant musicians of the next generation: from the "Cool School" and West Coast stylists Konitz and Mulligan, to the giant Coltrane, the fusion generation and today's contemporary jazz giants. The best of them played with Miles Davis.

This page: John Coltrane's Herculean stamina (it was not unknown for him to improvise continuously on a tune for more than an hour) and his still-unsurpassed saxophone virtuosity combined with his religious convictions and spiritual themes of his music to make him a complex jazz icon. A gentle man, he touched people with his personal modesty and terrified them with his music. His classic quartet, with pianist McCoy Tyner *(top right)*, bassist Jimmy Garrison and drummer Elvin Jones *(below)* remains one of the most influential groups in jazz. Their records *A Love Supreme* (1965) and *Crescent* (1964) are essential jazz highlights of the decade. Coltrane's final years (before his tragic death in 1967, two months before his 41st birthday) would be spent playing some of the period's most intense free jazz. Today, in San Francisco, there is a church where John Coltrane is worshipped as a christ. ●

DAVID REDFERN

Above: McCoy Tyner's dramatic chord voicings and driving, intense style were a cornerstone of the John Coltrane Quartet. He remains one of the finest pianists in contemporary jazz. ●

Right: For a brief period in 1961, Eric Dolphy made the John Coltrane Quartet a quintet. An utterly individual improviser, Dolphy developed a virtuoso technique on alto saxophone, flute and the difficult but effective bass clarinet. He soloed in a style that had roots in the pure bebop of Charlie Parker, but was broken up by dramatic, startling intervallic leaps and vocal effects. The results were sometimes passionate, sometimes humorous, but always compelling. He made a lot of great music in bassist Charles Mingus' band, and collaborated with saxophonist/arranger Oliver Nelson on a series of masterpieces, most notably *The Blues and the Abstract Truth*. As a leader, he left some of the finest recordings of the period, including his *Live at the Five Spot* albums, and his experimental *Out to Lunch*. ●

CHUCK STEWART

MILESTONES:

McCOY TYNER
IN INTERVIEW

"The evolution of my style had a lot to do with who I was playing with. Basically, how you hear the music has to come from within you, but you also have to be in the right environment in order to do that, and I had to be playing the kind of music that I was playing with John (Coltrane) in order to play that way. It was an opportunity to develop. I was hearing these sounds when I was a teenager, but I didn't really have too much of an opportunity until I joined John to implement them. He could do a lot of different things with the harmonic space my voicings left him. And I did a lot of moving around. There's no system involved, you just have to be able to hear what's going on and what fits what. You don't have time to implement any system. The whole thing was constantly moving. There was tremendous interplay in that band. Very intuitive.

We didn't rehearse that much. I remember rehearsing six or seven times, and that was just because new music was introduced. We reached a point where there were no chords at all, he'd bring a scale in and we'd create chords out of those notes and just move as we went along. There was no set form. It was an amazing lesson in listening and responding and respect for one another. There are a lot of lessons in playing this music, not only from a disciplinary point of view, but also being able to respond to someone else's ideas and have respect for that person."

DAVID REDFERN

Above: Andrew Hill was one of the most daring pianists of the period and, despite a clear gift for jazz composition, often teetered on the brink of freedom. ●

CHUCK STEWART

Above: Joe Henderson's warm, clear tenor saxophone style was one of the great finds of the 1960s. Henderson could play "out," but he always made sense. ●

Below: An inventive, powerful improviser, Sam Rivers stamped everything from the blues to the avant-garde with his own musical personality. He remains an underrated voice. ●

DAVID REDFERN

DAVID REDFERN

Above: Big band composer George Russell is one of jazz's most important theorists. His brilliant 1961 *Ezz-thetics* featured saxophonist Eric Dolphy. ●

DAVID REDFERN

Above: An eclectic, forward-looking vibraphone player, Bobby Hutcherson could be spiky and percussive, or warm and lyrical. He contributed to some of the most important sessions of the period, including Dolphy's *Out to Lunch* and Hill's *Point of Departure*. ●

MILESTONES:
SOME CLASSIC POST-BOP RECORDINGS

As the 1950s turned into the 1960s, the trend toward modal jazz, rather than the more harmonically regulated hard-bop, precipitated a fascinating period of experimentation. Not strictly free jazz, but deliberately loose and creative in its conception, it resulted in some of the most fascinating record dates of the 1960s.

Miles Davis: *Miles Smiles* (Columbia) Davis' classic 1960s quartet, with tenor saxophonist Wayne Shorter, pianist Herbie Hancock, bassist Ron Carter and drummer Tony Williams, was one of the most daring and spontaneous bands of the period. *Miles Smiles* features Shorter's beautiful blues waltz *Footprints*.

Eric Dolphy: *Out There* (Original Jazz Classics) This alto saxophonist, flutist and bass clarinetist based his approach on Charlie Parker's, but extended it to include passages of startling dissonance and huge, energetic leaps between notes. A genuine virtuoso, he sounds as exciting and insurgent today as ever.

John Coltrane: *My Favorite Things* (Atlantic) Saxophonist Coltrane transformed mediocre popular songs into vehicles for some of the most profound performances in jazz history. Here, *My Favorite Things* becomes an intense, almost religious, celebration of life.

McCoy Tyner: *The Real McCoy* (Blue Note) Not the most original title, but a true Blue Note masterpiece. Pianist Tyner took time off from the ground-breaking John Coltrane Quartet to record this absorbing modal outing with fellow Coltrane sideman Elvin Jones on drums, bassist Ron Carter and saxophonist Joe Henderson.

Andrew Hill: *Point of Departure* (Blue Note) Still an underrated pianist, Hill plays with a challenging, fractured style. This 1960s classic represents some of his finest work, in stellar company including saxophonists Eric Dolphy and Joe Henderson.

Below top: A gifted multi-instrumentalist, Yusef Lateef plays a host of Eastern instruments, in addition to the tenor saxophone and the flute. ●

Below bottom: A trumpeter with a bold technique and rich sound, Woody Shaw played on Eric Dolphy's 1963 *Iron Man* and organist Larry Young's 1965 masterpiece *Unity*. ●

Above: A troubled and tempestuous jazz genius with a personality even more complex than his music, Charles Mingus was one of the finest bassists jazz has ever seen, and undoubtedly one of its very best composers. In a career that stretched from a stint in the Louis Armstrong Orchestra to recognition as one of the leaders of the avant-garde, he worked with Duke Ellington and Charlie Parker before embarking on a career as a leader. His own series of bands, featuring, at various times, saxophonists Jackie McLean, Eric Dolphy, Roland Kirk, George Adams and usually powered along by drummer Dannie Richmond, fused complicated, unorthodox structures with the most soulful and blues-drenched improvisation imaginable.

Unpredictable, to say the least, and painfully sensitive to racism and condescension, Mingus could be pushed by frustration to the end of his fuse at any time. He is reputed to have attacked members of his band and members of the audience. *The Black Saint and the Sinner Lady* is an essential Mingus album, while his autobiography, *Beneath the Underdog*, is a fascinating and brilliantly written book. ●

Above: A cutting-edge pianist since the 1950s, Paul Bley played with Charlie Parker and Charles Mingus, and was one of the pioneers of free jazz. ●

Above and Right: His group with guitarist Jim Hall *(above)* was a West Coast jazz favorite, but in the early 1960s, reedsman Jimmy Giuffre collaborated with pianist Paul Bley and bassist Steve Swallow on a delicate and refined free jazz. ●

93

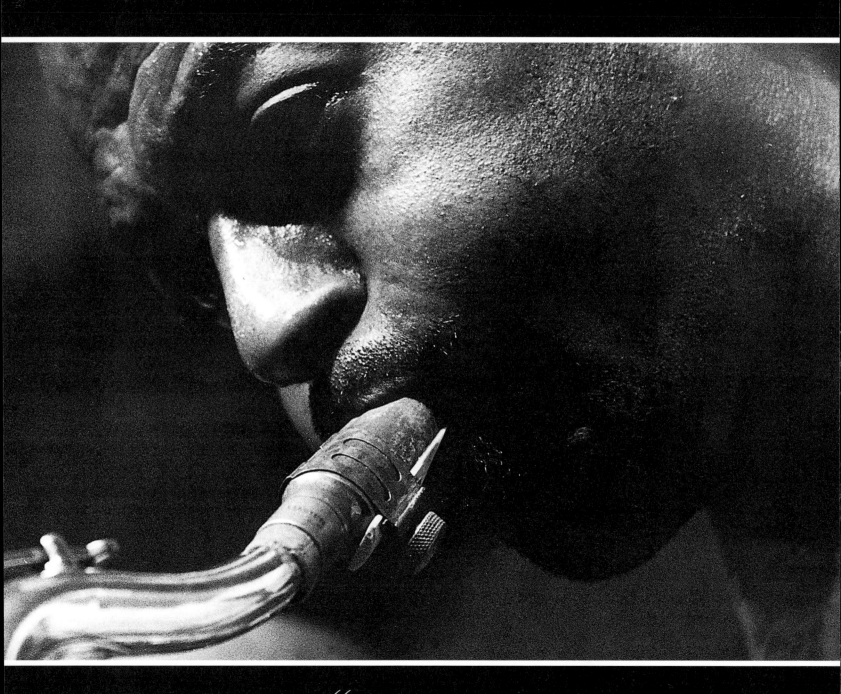

**" *Free at last, free at last*
Thank God Almighty, free at last "**

FREEDOM & POLITICS

I t seems strange how such a beautiful and almost naively straightfoward music could be met with such dissension. But the recordings that mark the dawn of the free jazz era – albums such as *The Shape of Jazz to Come* and *Change of the Century* – made shy, Texan alto saxophonist Ornette Coleman a figure of fierce controversy.

By 1958, pianist Cecil Taylor had already been practicing a fractured, *staccato* and shocking style. Another pianist, Lennie Tristano, had improvised intense solo music from nothing, and bandleader Sun Ra had been busy making strange and daring sounds. It was Coleman, however, and his piano-less quartet, that launched the free jazz era, releasing a musical force that would be picked up by a talented group of politically-aware musicians, and played throughout the years of the black civil rights movement and beyond. Jazz was no longer the accessible and popular sound it had been during the swing era, but it was right at the forefront of the avant-garde.

Left: Fire music, from Archie Shepp. ●

Above: Free jazz king, Pharoah Sanders. ●

This page: Don Cherry's little "pocket trumpet" produced one of the most distinctive sounds in post-war jazz. Fragile and attractive, it was a feature of Ornette Coleman's classic free jazz quartet, and was heard in a world music context in the decades to come.

Quick-thinking and instinctive, Don Cherry was the perfect partner for Ornette Coleman. On the series of classic recordings they made together, his fractured but boppy lines carry just as much force as Coleman's own bluesy extemporization. He recorded with John Coltrane and Albert Ayler, and, by the end of the decade, was experimenting with eastern forms and instruments. ●

DAVID REDFERN

DAVID REDFERN

This page: Bearded and bohemian, controversial alto saxophonist (and even more controversial trumpeter and violinist) Ornette Coleman saw in the free jazz era. His series of albums for the Atlantic label rewrote the rules of jazz improvisation. In place of chord sequences, his pianoless quartet relied on a close group dynamic, in which the soloist and the bassist invented the harmony as they went along, in a continuous creative dialogue. Not everyone was impressed, and in the early 1960s Coleman was regularly dismissed as a charlatan. His music, however, was just too beautiful not to be influential. Coleman was an inspired composer of tunes, too. *Lonely Woman* and *Congeniality* on *The Shape of Jazz to Come*, and *Blues Connotation* on *This is Our Music* are essential listening. ●

MILESTONES:

ORNETTE COLEMAN
IN INTERVEIW

"I was born in the South, in Texas, and when I got a saxophone I started teaching myself how to play it. And fortunately I was in a city, so I heard many people who were playing jazz passing through on their way to California. When I started playing professionally, I was playing mostly R&B because I was a teenager, and the music I encountered mostly every day was R&B. I met a young man in my home town who was playing bebop. Bebop musicians were making two chords out of any one chord. When I found that out, I started thinking, 'If this is true, let's see how it works in relationship to other chords.' But I found out it wasn't something that allows you to step outside that, it only allows you to make an extension of it. When I realized that, I figured that if I didn't think of a sequence I wouldn't have to resort to any standard chord changes.

I had a promoter call me up saying he wanted to put on a concert of my free jazz. I said, 'OK,' and assembled a cast of people and went to Ohio. Now this is a true story. There was a big sign on one of the largest theaters there, saying 'Free Jazz Tonight.' You know what happened? Five thousand people turned up but they wouldn't buy any tickets! They were thinking like 'Free Candy!' The musicians sued me and I had a terrible time. But when the free jazz movement was in existence, it just had such an impact on people who wanted to play the way they played."

97

Below: Revolutionary drummer Rashied Ali was a pioneer of "pulse drumming," a complex style in which the beat is "implied." He worked with John Coltrane. ●

Below: Saxophonist and writer Archie Shepp was recommended to the Impulse label by John Coltrane (with whom he briefly collaborated). His 1965 *Fire Music*, with its *Poem for Malcom X*, reflected the political motivation behind much of Shepp's music and literature. ●

Above: Pharoah Sanders' ferocious saxophone style involved wailing, honking, squawking and blasting. He was encouraged by John Coltrane, and together they toured in one of the most uncompromising units of the mid-1960s. ●

Above: John Coltrane's second wife, pianist and harp player Alice Coltrane, joined the saxophonist's band in 1965, replacing McCoy Tyner, and led her own groups after his death. ●

This page: In the late 1950s, pianist Cecil Taylor was already experimenting with his own fragmented and percussive vision of free improvisation. Very different in character to both Ornette Coleman's music and John Coltrane's, Taylor's gesture-orientated improvisations were rooted in the physicality of playing the piano. He had studied both classical piano and percussion, and seemed to combine both activities, developing a startlingly fast-fingered and hard-hitting approach to the keyboard. Despite harsh economic setbacks, by the mid-1960s he was developing a reputation as a musical giant-in-the-making. He has indeed played a key role in the avant-garde ever since. He is a wild and visually compelling performer. ●

99

DAVID REDFERN

DAVID REDFERN

This page: Hidden in a rough, wailing tone, the awesome beauty of Albert Ayler's music can take a little finding, and the 1960s' jazz scene was just not ready for him. While playing in rhythm and blues bands, he made his own celebrated first record, *My Name is Albert Ayler*, in Sweden. Returning to the States, he led a series of bands for which he remains remembered today, playing a sometimes joyous, sometimes excruciatingly severe and ponderous mixture of spirituals, marches and folk songs, with a wild *vibrato* and a tone that shuddered with emotional extremity. Some listeners heard in Ayler's music an artistic awakening; others accused him of not being able to play the saxophone. Tragically, he was found drowned in New York's East River in 1970. ●

REDFERNS

DAVID REDFERN

DAVID REDFERN

Above: Sun Ra lived a myth of his own invention. He called his big band the "Arkestra" and claimed to have been born on Saturn and sent to Earth on a mission. The Arkestra sang songs with "intergalactic" themes, and dressed in odd, shiny space suits. Ra's eccentricity led to a misunderstanding on the part of some commentators, who rejected his presentation as madness and/or comedy – but Sun Ra was extending a complicated African-American political metaphor relating to ancient civilizations. Musically, the band was ahead of its time, prefiguring both free jazz and fusion (Ra was one of the first jazz musicians to use a synthesizer). Some of the postwar period's finest improvisers, including saxophonists Marshall Allen and John Gilmore, remained committed to Ra's Arkestra for several decades. ●

MILESTONES:
THE UNSUNG FREEDOM FIGHTERS

According to jazz lore, alto saxophonist Ornette Coleman invented free jazz in 1959. However, while Coleman may have been the movement's single most important pioneer, forward-looking improvisers had been experimenting with freedom ever since the late 1940s.

Charlie Parker: An instinctive improviser if ever there was one, the inventor of the modern jazz bebop language was not averse to the occasional flight of fancy, as his live recordings testify. Listen to his *Bird at St. Nick's* album for an example of a musician who was far ahead of his time.

Jackie McLean: Alto saxophonist McLean was one of the first generation of Charlie Parker copyists. After joining the Blue Note label in the late 1950s, he began to push past the boundaries of harmony. He later became influenced by, and worked with, Coleman.

Lennie Tristano: A fascinating pianist and theorist, Tristano was the "cool jazz" movement's figurehead: a difficult player with some unorthodox views. Rarities, such as his 1953 piano improvisation *Descent into the Maelstrom*, reveal a startling free improviser, years ahead of his time; indeed, Tristano had been experimenting with group improvisation since 1949.

Sun Ra: One of the most eccentric figures of jazz, key-boardist and bandleader Sun Ra was not only one of the first jazz musicians to experiment with electronic instruments, he was also playing something bordering on freedom back in the mid-1950s.

Cecil Taylor: Taylor developed into perhaps the most celebrated pianist of the avant-garde. His percusive, dramatic and gesture-oriented approach dates back as far as 1958. As the years passed he would become a figure of unprecedented fire and vision on the free scene.

Left and Far left: Not only could the extraordinary Roland Rahsaan Kirk play this many saxophones at once, he could play them with ferocious virtuosity and originality. ●

Above and Right: A co-founder of the brilliant Art Ensemble of Chicago, and one of the Windy City's most powerful saxophonists, master composer and improviser Roscoe Mitchell blew onto the jazz scene in the 1960s. ●

Above: Tough-toned Argentinian tenor saxophonist, Gato Barbieri. ●

Above: Bassist Malachi Favors blends mysticism with his music. ●

Above: The Art Ensemble of Chicago, with white-coated trumpeter Lester Bowie, saxophonists Roscoe Mitchell and Joseph Jarman, bassist Malachi Favors and drummer Famoudou Don Moye, was formed in 1968. Painting their faces and wearing African garb, they created a mixture of jazz, rhythm and blues and theater, but preferred the term "Great Black Music." It often was, and still is. ●

Left: Pianist and composer Muhal Richard Abrams played hard-bop at first, but formed The Experimental Band in 1961. He founded the AACM in 1965, helping an entire generation of forward-looking musicians to find a voice, and has been a vital figure in Chicago's avant-garde ever since. ●

Above: Lester Bowie uses old techniques in new music. ●

❝ *I thought it would be good if I could get all these young people together listening to my music
and digging the groove.* **❞**

DAVID REDFERN

FUSION:
HARD & SOFT

B y the end of the 1960s, jazz was facing the biggest onslaught it would ever have to suffer. The economic powerhouse that was rock was converting jazz clubs into rock venues, the major record labels were busy capitalizing on the new, lucrative youth market, and jazz musicians were finding it increasingly difficult to make ends meet.

Once again on the cutting edge of contemporary tastes, Miles Davis released a series of albums that would revolutionize the sound of jazz, shifting his musicians onto electric instruments, directing his drummers toward funk-rock rhythms and, by the mid-1970s, choosing his new sidemen from the worlds of rock and rhythm and blues.

The fusion of jazz with other forms was not completely unheard of (the music itself was the result of a fusion of different styles, and it had already absorbed Latin rhythms from Cuban salsa and Brazilian samba). The jazz-rock movement was, however, far-reaching, stretching from the hard, thrashy sound of drummer Billy Cobham to the soft and ethereal textures of Pat Metheny.

Left: Heavy-duty fusion drummer Billy Cobham. ●

Above: Herbie Hancock, the funkiest man on keyboards. ●

This page: After the sparse minimalism of *In a Silent Way* and the spooky jazz-rock of *Bitches Brew*, Miles Davis began the 1970s firmly committed to the new electric sound. Most of the leading figures in what was yet to be called "fusion" appeared with Davis at one time or another. By 1975, he had pushed his music further and further out, until he was playing a raucous, almost completely improvised music over hard-rock rhythms, even distorting his trumpet tone with effects pedals. Then – following a car crash and a series of personal problems – he announced his retirement.

His comeback in 1981 marked the start of another highly creative period, in which Davis would forge a new, softer, pop-influenced sound, and once again surround himself with the finest up-and-coming players. Records such as *Tutu* and *Amandla* (from 1986 and 1989, respectively) still sound utterly contemporary.

Despite a notoriously spikey personality, Miles Davis was a marvelously popular musician, and an icon. His death in 1991 left a permanent hollow in the jazz world. ●

DAVID REDFERN

This page: John McLaughlin was born in England, and moved to New York to work with ex-Miles Davis drummer Tony Williams. But he was called up by Davis himself, and contributed to the trumpeter's early fusion classics *In a Silent Way* and *Bitches Brew*. McLaughlin's own band – The Mahavishnu Orchestra *(left)* – was a zealous fusion powerhouse, driven along by drummer Billy Cobham. It was noisy, virtuosic and over-the-top, but short-lived. He replaced it in the mid-1970s with Shakti, featuring Indian violinist L. Shankar and tabla player Zakir Hussain.

McLaughlin's penchant for customized guitars included a guitar with two necks *(left)*, and a special instrument with raised strings which he could play like a sitar. Since the 1970s, he has toured in an all-star guitar trio, led his own groups, and collaborated with orchestras. He remains one of the finest contemporary jazz guitarists. ●

MARC MARNIE

This page: When Herbie Hancock left Miles Davis at the end of the 1960s, he formed his own fusion band and focused on the newly invented synthesizer. As his music grew funkier, it became more popular, and his 1973 *Headhunters* album – a brilliant, catchy blend of jazz improvisation and dancefloor beats – was one of the biggest jazz-related commercial successes ever. A series of disco-oriented projects followed, before Hancock returned to the jazz mainstream in the 1980s. ●

Right: A gifted bebop guitarist and a soulful vocalist, George Benson was a regular feature of the album charts in the 1970s, with records such as the funky, Grammy-winning *Breezin'*. ●

Above: Tony Williams left Miles Davis in the late 1960s to form his own fusion band, Lifetime. ●

Above: Joe Zawinul also played with Davis, but left in 1971 to co-found Weather Report. ●

Above: Popular fusion band Weather Report was the brainchild of ex-Davis colleagues Joe Zawinul and Wayne Shorter. Their music ranged from textural electronics to Latin funk. ●

MILESTONES:
MOVERS AND SHAKERS OF THE FUSION MOVEMENT

Miles Davis incorporated electric instruments into his band for the first time in 1968 on the album *Miles in the Sky*. By 1972, he was deeply involved in a loose, fiery, new music, formed around rock rhythms, electric instruments, and world music percussion.

Chick Corea had been active in hard-bop and Latin music before his electric piano became a cornerstone of Miles Davis' new sound. His Return to Forever bands were some of the most popular fusion acts of the 1970s, and his Elektric Band a key group in the 1980s.

Herbie Hancock parted company with Davis in 1968 to set out on his own. Where Davis had leaned toward rock, Hancock fused with funk, recording a series of jazz-funk classics, including the deeply catchy *Headhunters* — the best-selling jazz album of all time.

Weather Report was formed by keyboardist Joe Zawinul and saxophonist Wayne Shorter after leaving Davis in 1971. There were several incarnations, but the band was always considered an important fusion act, gaining huge popularity at the beginning of the 1980s.

Dreams prefigured the immensely popular Brecker Brothers band, and, in 1970, featured trumpet and tenor saxophone partners Randy and Michael Brecker, with top jazz-rock drummer Billy Cobham and guitarist John Abercrombie. The group disbanded in 1973.

The Brecker Brothers recorded some of the most exciting jazz-funk of the 1970s. Randy (trumpet) and Michael (tenor saxophone) were joined by top session musicians, including alto saxophonist David Sanborn.

Steps was formed by vibraphonist Mike Mainieri in 1979. It became a fusion legend, and featured drummer Peter Erskine and saxophonist Michael Brecker.

DAVID REDFERN

Above: A cult hero among electric bassists, Jaco Pastorius began what was to be a short but stellar fusion career in the mid-1970s when he recorded with Pat Metheny on the guitarist's first record for the ECM label. In 1976, he was invited to join the already well-established fusion band Weather Report, and he remains commonly associated with this period. The album *Heavy Weather* featured the bassist's stunning technique, and it became one of the group's most popular records. He left to form his own band, Word of Mouth, in 1980.

Jaco Pastorius was an incredible virtuoso, and thrilled audiences with his ostentatious stage demeanor. Unfortunately, he suffered from alcoholism, and was tragically killed in a brawl outside a club in 1987. ●

This page: Chick Corea played with Miles Davis between 1968 and 1970, contributing the lovely, watery tones of the Fender Rhodes electric piano. During the 1970s, he led three bands called Return to Forever, playing music that ranged from animated Latin fusion to hard-hitting jazz-rock. The first album under the group's name, entitled simply *Return to Forever* and released on ECM in 1972, featured percussionist Airto Moreira, vocalist Flora Purim and bassist Stanley Clarke; it is an essential album from the period. In the 1980s, Corea achieved huge popularity with two intense, virtuoso versions of the same band, called the Akoustic Band and the Elektric Band, both featuring fast-fingered bassist John Patitucci *(pictured with Corea, left)*.

As a keyboardist and pianist, Chick Corea is truly one of the jazz greats. As a bandleader, he has shaped the course of fusion music for three decades. ●

DAVID REDFERN

ANDREW PUTLER

DANY GIGNOUX

DAVID REDFERN

Above: Ornette Coleman played his own style of free fusion, with a new electric group he called Prime Time. ●

Above: Counting down… the extraordinary fusion sticksman, Billy Cobham. ●

Above: John Abercrombie started in Cobham's fusion band Spectrum, but came to specialize in a softer style. ●

Above: Hits like the beautiful *Everybody Loves the Sunshine* made vibraphonist Roy Ayers a jazz-funk favorite. ●

EBET ROBERTS

MICHAEL LINSSEN

Above: In the 1970s, hard-bop trumpeter Donald Byrd formed a popular funk band called The Blackbyrds. Today he collaborates with rappers. ●

Above: Versatile guitarist Pat Metheny *(center)* specializes in an atmospheric, texture-conscious jazz-rock, and has utilized the strengths of the guitar-synth. ●

DAVID REDFERN

Left: The Brecker Brothers (Randy on trumpet and Michael on tenor saxophone) set new standards of virtuosity in the fusion scene. Their partnership produced some of the fastest moving and most advanced jazz-rock of the 1970s. ●

PAUL BERGEN

Above: Stanley Clarke's awesome virtuosity extends to both the double and the electric bass. After an orthodox jazz apprenticeship with the likes of Horace Silver, Art Blakey and Dexter Gordon, Clarke joined Corea's first, and best, Return to Forever lineup, collaborating with drummer/percussionist Airto Moreira. This was a magical rhythm section partnership. He stayed with Corea until 1977, before working as a leader and in collaboration with keyboardist/composer George Duke. Stanley Clarke remains simply one of the most exciting bassists around. ●

MILESTONES:
FUSION—
THE NEW INSTRUMENTS

Brass: Faced in the early 1970s with the huge commercial popularity of rock, and feeling increasingly drawn to the music himself, Miles Davis sought ways of aping the anguished improvisations of Jimi Hendrix. He began experimenting with new methods of electric amplification, employing a wah-wah pedal to distort the trumpet's tone.

Reeds: It was not until the 1980s, and the invention of the Electric Wind Instrument (EWI), that saxophonists were given a significant new "toy." The EWI, in the hands of a skilled technician such as Michael Brecker, combines a massive range with an unlimited array of sounds — some synthetic, some sampled.

Keyboards: The Hammond organ had already enjoyed a jazz "authenticity" for some time when an explosion of synthesizers and keyboards presented pianists with a whole new bag of tricks. The attractive, watery tones of the Fender Rhodes electric piano became a classic fusion sound, associated primarily with Chick Corea.

Guitar: Rock put the guitar right at the center of youthful musical activity, and the result was an explosion of virtuoso technicians, who could play lines with the speed of a saxophonist.

Bass: The bass guitar, directly amplified and less cumbersome than the double bass, increased in favor. Jaco Pastorius, bassist with Weather Report, set new standards of virtuosity on the instrument.

Drums: Kits got bigger, and drummers got louder. The bass drum and the snare once again began to carry the beat, as drummers lifted, and adapted, rock and funk drumming patterns. The drum machine and sampler, borrowed from contemporary dance music, would soon begin to make their presence felt.

❝ *Music ...is a way of stepping through the wall to another place where things are, in some ways, more straightforward.* **❞**

AVANT-GARDE & EURO JAZZ

Left: Dancing to the tune of a different soprano saxophone ...and British free-sax genius Evan Parker. ●

Above: Noisy European improvisers – Dutch drummer Han Bennink, German saxophonist Peter Brötzmann and German trombonist Albert Mangelsdorff. ●

A largely improvised music, jazz was built on democratic principles that appealed to musicians outside of the United States too. Europe, with its history of musical experimentation, took to free improvisation in particular; and, in the 1960s, intense pockets of activity began to develop. In London, a Yorkshire-born session guitarist called Derek Bailey began to collaborate with a group of musicians organized around the Little Theatre Club. One of them, drummer John Stevens, a tireless advocate of free improvisation, set up the Spontaneous Music Ensemble – a group that, with different members, would specialize in a dynamic, Ornette Coleman-influenced freebop. Bailey continued working with Stevens until the drummer's death in 1994. His own series of festivals, known as "Company Week," featured some of the world's finest free improvisers, and could result in challenging but startlingly powerful music.

Meanwhile, European jazz musicians were rediscovering their own folk music. Manfred Eicher's ECM label, launched in 1969, featured both European and leading American musicians, but grew to characterize an intense, atmospheric blend of European folk, classical music, jazz and fusion. ▶

DAVID REDFERN

Above: Ferocious German saxophonist Peter Brötzmann shot to notoriety with *Machine Gun* – his 1968 free-sax ruckus. In three decades, no-one has surpassed this European free jazz classic in terms of sheer fury or musical brutality. ●

PETER SYMES

Above: Dutch saxophonist Willem Breuker and his madcap Kollektief. Breuker played on Brötzmann's *Machine Gun*, but specializes in his own mixture of complex composition, Dadaist improvisation, comedy and jazz. ●

PETER SYMES

Left: Evan Parker is probably the most advanced saxophonist in the world. One of the pioneers of free improvisation, he played on Brötzmann's *Machine Gun* session. Currently, he specializes in an astonishing solo saxophone style that involves split tones, harmonics and odd shadings, played at breakneck speed and with the aid of circular breathing – often giving the impression of more than one saxophone being played at once. ●

Right: British guitarist Derek Bailey has done more than any other musician to further understanding of what can be a tricky and challenging music. His book, *Improvisation: Its Nature and Practise in Music*, is essential reading. For 17 years he ran the international improvised music festival, Company Week. His own guitar playing is full of surprises, ranging from the most delicate articulation imaginable to thick, intense strumming. ●

DANY GIGNOUX

This page: German trombonist Albert Mangelsdorff has played every type of jazz, but is a key figure in the European avant-garde. In the early 1970s he perfected a technique that enabled him to play one note while singing another simultaneously. ●

MILESTONES:

DEREK BAILEY

IN HIS OWN WORDS

"I used to enjoy playing conventional jazz and I used to play it a lot. But the longer I played and the more satisfactory it got for me, the more unsatisfactory it got for other people, because I was looking for things that would never be there. And if I found them, I wasn't really playing the music.

Improvised music's connection with jazz is umbilical and undeniable. But when the cord is cut, when it gets away from being jazz, that's when its potential is really attractive.

I like the early stages of relationships in free playing. They always seem to be the richest to me. For some players, the real rewards come later, when they've got this homogeneous solid group thing. I've never been attracted by that. I like these early stages before the music solidifies into being a style. The early stages might last five days, and that can be interesting. I find that after five or six days, they seem to find a limit to their fertile common ground.

One of the great things about group improvisation, is that it's no one person's music. I don't know that it happens in any other art – I don't see how it can. But here it's essentially symbiotic – it can't work any other way, because you've got all these people working together with no demands on them, other than they've got to produce something with the others."

Above: Keyboardist Vyacheslav Ganelin, Russia's most celebrated improviser, and leader of the famous Ganelin Trio. ●

Right: Just one of Fred Frith's unconventional guitar techniques. Frith co-founded left-field rock band Henry Cow, and currently plays an exciting mix of rock-informed free improvisation. ●

Above: Steve Lacy was inspired by Sidney Bechet, but worked with Cecil Taylor! A soprano saxophonist with a big, blunt sound, he has played everything from Dixieland to free improvisation. Born in New York, he relocated to Europe in the 1960s. ●

Above: American pianist Marilyn Crispell is influenced by the great Cecil Taylor, and is one of Braxton's favorite musical collaborators. ●

Above: Eccentric free-sax star Anthony Braxton grew out of Chicago's AACM. He is a master of the solo saxophone improvisation, and his compositions have included some pieces titled with odd diagrams, and others written for several orchestras to play at once. ●

Above: Norwegian tenor and soprano saxophonist Jan Garbarek has a dry, compelling sound with roots in both jazz and folk. ●

Above: Originally a fusioneer, Czech bassist Miroslav Vitous co-founded Weather Report, but contributed to ECM's folk-slanted sound. ●

Above: Eberhard Weber, a brilliant German bassist and ECM recording artist. ●

Right: Finnish drummer Edward Vesala grew up playing tangos at dances. His current band, Sound and Fury, retains elements of his own folk music alongside jazz and modern classical music. ●

MILESTONES:
THE ECM LABEL
RECOMMENDED RECORDINGS

Launched in Munich in 1969, ECM (Edition for Contemporary Music) has grown into one of the world's most successful independent jazz labels. Still run by its exacting founder Manfred Eicher, ECM has been of fundamental importance in the creation of "European" jazz, and is well known for its hermetic, hi-fi sound.

Jan Garbarek: *Eventyr* (1980)
A bleak and moving mixture of adapted folk music and original tunes, led by prolific ECM recording artist Garbarek on saxophones, with guitarist John Abercrombie and percussionist Nana Vasconcelos.

Chick Corea: *Piano Improvisations Vols 1 & 2* (1971)
Just before his incarnation as one of fusion's premier bandleaders, Corea drew on classical music to make these two volumes of attractive solo-piano improvisations. In the early 1990s he toured internationally playing music from these ECM sides.

Keith Jarrett: *The Köln Concert* (1975)
ECM's best-selling album, this is the cult record by the label's cult pianist. A creative blend of contemporary jazz, classical music and folk, it is a deeply absorbing album, and continues to attract fans from all musical spheres.

Jan Garbarek: *Officium* (1994)
A modern classic, this brought Norwegian saxophonist Garbarek together with the respected Hilliard Ensemble early music choral group, for a program that skillfully mixed saxophone improvisation and Gregorian chant.

Eberhard Weber: *The Colours of Chloë* (1973)
Bassist Weber typifies the cool and sometimes austere European jazz sound with which the ECM label is commonly associated. *The Colours of Chloë*, with its clever mixture of strings and electronics, is a hauntingly atmospheric masterpiece.

> **The approval of the older jazz generation means everything to me...
> because they're my idols.**

JOSHUA REDMAN

EBET ROBERTS

JAZZ TODAY

The jazz scene went through a depression in the 1970s. The overwhelming popularity of rock made it virtually impossible for a musician to make a living playing acoustic jazz, and fusion was the order of the day.

Currently, however, jazz is thriving on an unprecedented eclecticism. New fusions include mixtures of jazz and hiphop, African music, Latin music, country and pop, while revivalist movements have spawned some brilliant musicians specializing in old-style swing and bop.

The musical establishment – once a bastion of "art music" snobbery and exclusivity – has opened its doors to jazz improvisers. Today's jazz giants tend to learn their trade on college jazz courses, rather than from the hit-and-miss jam sessions of the big band scene. Some people feared that the teaching of improvisation would have a homogenizing effect on jazz musicians. So far, however, the best players have shown a level of individuality and originality equal to the rising stars of the past.

From a New Orleans hybrid, to a sophisticated, profound, international musical language… the heroic history of jazz is one of the most compelling tales of the 20th century.

Left: Innovative alto saxophonist Kenny Garrett blows up a storm. ●

Left inset and Above: Young man and a horn …well-connected tenor talent Joshua Redman (his father, Dewey Redman, played saxophone with Ornette Coleman) made a massive splash in the 1990s. ●

125

DAVID REDFERN

This page: Certainly the single most important jazz musician to have materialized in decades, and a name inseparable from the revival of fortunes enjoyed by jazz since the 1980s, trumpeter Wynton Marsalis comes from one of New Orleans' most musical families. He has carved himself a unique position as musical spokesperson for the new generation of ambitious and well-schooled jazz musicians. ●

BOB WILLOUGHBY

Above: Tough, bluesy and prolific, tenor saxophonist and bass clarinetist David Murray takes after the Hawkins, Rollins and Ayler tradition. ●

Above: Perhaps the last great talent discovered by Miles Davis, Kenny Garrett was a feature of the trumpeter's final band. ●

Above: Keith Jarrett's intense and lyrical piano improvisations, accompanied by the groaning of a musician in the ecstasies of inspiration, are the most influential sound in jazz piano today. ●

Left: Contemporary jazz pianist Geri Allen played in Coleman's M-Base group in the 1980s, and has a sparkling, melodic touch. ●

Right: In the 1980s, alto saxophonist Steve Coleman invented a new, complex, polyrhythmic funk called M-Base. He is currently one of the most startlingly original voices on the instrument. ●

127

STUART NICHOLSON

Above: After playing a pivotal role in Ornette Coleman's original free jazz quartet, and making waves with his own Liberation Music Orchestra, Charlie Haden remains one of the finest living jazz bassists. ●

EBET ROBERTS

Above: The finest singer of her generation, Cassandra Wilson worked with Steve Coleman in the early days of M-Base, but sounds best on her own deep and smoky, blues-soaked recordings. ●

DAVID REDFERN

Above: Chick Corea has spent more time on the acoustic piano, playing a complex and involved post-bop. He plays his own atmospheric compositions, as well as music by Thelonious Monk and Bud Powell, and leads a fine band featuring saxophonist Bob Berg. ●

DANY GIGNOUX

Left: Bob Berg – one of the most advanced tenor and soprano saxophonists in the world – and a quarter of one of Chick Corea's most gripping recent bands. ●

MILESTONES:
JAZZ SINGERS TODAY

Still seen largely as a female domain, the jazz vocalist's art was somewhat sidelined during the music's great postwar revolutions, and has not kept the frantic pace of development associated with instrumental jazz. But a look at four of the music's more popular contemporary vocalists shows just how the scene has compensated with a richness and eclecticism that is sometimes forgotten.

Sheila Jordan: A devotee, during the 1950s, of Charlie Parker, Jordan based her style on the bebop model, and studied with Charles Mingus and Lennie Tristano. She has played with many of the world's top contemporary jazz instrumentalists, and continues to perform with an amazing virtuosity.

Dianne Reeves: A popular Blue Note recording artist, Reeves made her name in the 1980s, but has spent the intervening years splitting her time between jazz and soul. Her best work reveals an impeccable rhythmic sense; and recently she has used elements of world music to introduce a fresh sound.

Cassandra Wilson: One of the most gifted vocalists to emerge in a long time, Wilson spent the 1980s involved with musicians from the tricky, crypto-funk M-Base project. Her more recent records for the Blue Note label, however, have been ground-breaking blends of contemporary jazz and Delta blues — with her deep and distinctive delivery being accompanied by novel small-group arrangements.

Abbey Lincoln: Active since the late 1950s, Lincoln's reputation stems from the 1960s, when she collaborated with drummer Max Roach on a series of all-star dates. A politically driven singer and lyricist, she has a plain but compelling approach to a song, and is heard to good effect on Roach's 1960 *We Insist! Freedom Now Suite*. In the 1960s she combined jazz with work as a successful movie actress.

Above and Top right: Since the death of Miles Davis in 1991 and Dizzy Gillespie in 1993, Sonny Rollins is in many ways the last remaining jazz giant. Still improvising like the master that he is, he clips a microphone onto the bell of his saxophone, and paces the stage, producing torrents of notes and playing a mixture of lesser-known show tunes, bop classics and calypsos. ●

Left: Born in Canada but now living in London, trumpeter and flügelhorn player Kenny Wheeler plays with an attractive, bleak tone and introverted, angular style. ●

Below: The bad boy of the alto, saxophonist John Zorn is an explosive, subversive jazz talent, responsible for some of New York's wildest free sessions. ●

MILESTONES:
JAZZ RECORD LABELS TODAY

The rise of the large entertainment corporations has meant that many of the traditional jazz labels have lost their independence, while elsewhere small labels specializing in classic or early recordings have sprung up to deal in old rarities. (Such labels have often been quick to take advantage of lapsed copyrights.) But some labels still offer clues about their music. The following list identifies a handful of labels associated with each of the popular jazz genres.

New Orleans/Dixieland jazz: BBC, Affinity, Classics, Bluebird, JSP, Fountain, Storyville.

Big band swing: Bluebird, Affinity, MCA, Hep, Classics, Vintage Jazz Classics.

Bebop: Spotlite, Savoy, Blue Note, Vogue.

Hard-bop: Original Jazz Classics, Blue Note, Black Lion, Verve.

West Coast: Original Jazz Classics, Pacific Jazz, Capitol, Atlantic.

Post-bop: Blue Note, Impulse!, Atlantic, Columbia.

Free jazz: Blue Note, ESP, Atlantic, Impulse!, Strata East, Candid, Soul Note, Leo.

Fusion/jazz funk: GRP, Columbia, Blue Note, Atlantic, ECM, Talkin' Loud, Mo'Wax.

Free improvisation: Incus, Leo, FMP.

Neobop: Muse, Candid, Enja, Concord.

Contemporary jazz: JMT, Blue Note, Soul Note, ECM, Impulse!, GRP, Verve.

131

DAVID REDFERN

DAVID REDFERN

This page: One of the older musicians who enjoyed a renaissance during the 1980s jazz revival, tenor saxophonist Joe Henderson released his landmark Blue Note set *State of the Tenor Volumes 1 and 2.* Joining Verve, he made a series of Grammy Award-winning masterpieces in the 1990s. Henderson's mellow, burnished tone is currently one of the most beautiful sounds in jazz, and he is a masterful improviser. ●

Above: An incredible, fast-fingered virtuoso on the tenor saxophone, Michael Brecker is inspired by Coltrane, but influenced by the fusion scene. He is a titanic force on the instrument, and one of the busiest and most popular men in contemporary jazz. ●

Above: Dave Holland, an intricate acoustic bassist and innovative bandleader. ●

Above: Individualistic tenor sax talent, Joe Lovano. ●

Above: John Scofield, one of the finest guitarists in contemporary jazz. ●

Above: Drummer Peter Erskine works with the best of today's jazz and fusion soloists. ●

Above: Bill Frisell mixes jazz with country music and American classical music. ●

JAZZ HISTORY

F A M I L Y   T R E E

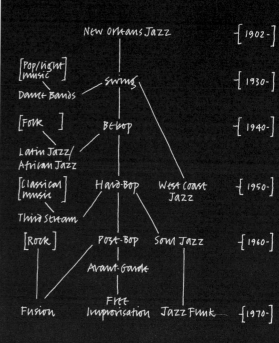

Jazz history hurtled outward from its New Orleans origins to the complexities of free improvisation in less than a lifetime, constantly fusing with other music to retain its vitality. Today, all of these forms are played in jazz clubs and concert halls across the globe.

133

INDEX
Page numbers in *italics* refer to illustrations

FURTHER READING

Campbell, James, ed. *The Picador Book of Blues and Jazz*. London: Picador, 1995.

Carr, Ian. *Miles Davis*. London: Quartet Books, 1982.

Cook, Richard & Morton, Brian, eds. *The Penguin Guide to Jazz on CD, LP & Cassette*. London: Penguin Books, 1992.

Crow, Bill. *Jazz Anecdotes*. New York: Oxford University Press, 1990.

Davis, Miles with Troupe, Quincy. *Miles - The Autobiography*. New York: Simon & Schuster, 1989.

Gelly, Dave. *Lester Young*. Tunbridge Wells: Spellmount Ltd, 1984.

Hasse, John Edward. *Beyond Category - The Life & Genius of Duke Ellington*. New York: Simon & Schuster, 1993.

Kernfled, Barry, ed. *The New Grove Dictionary of Jazz*. London: Macmillan Press Limited, 1994.

Larkin, Colin, ed. *The Guinness Who's Who of Jazz*. London: Guinness Publishing Ltd, 1992, revised 1995.

Litweiler, John. *The Freedom Principle - Jazz After 1958*. New York: Da Capo Press, 1984.

Lock, Graham. *Chasing the Vibration*. Exeter: Stride Publications, 1994.

Mingus, Charles. *Beneath the Underdog*. New York: Alfred A. Knopf Inc, 1971.

Pepper, Art & Laurie. *Straight Life - The Story of Art Pepper*. New York: Schirmer Books, 1979.

Perry, David. *Jazz Greats*. London: Phaidon Press Limited, 1996.

Russell, Ross. *Bird Lives*. London: Quartet Books, 1973.

Schuller, Gunther. *Early Jazz: its Roots and Musical Development*. Oxford: Oxford University Press, 1968.

Thomas, J. C. *Chasin' the Trane*. New York: Doubleday, 1975.

Wood, Ean. *Born to Swing*. London: Sanctuary Publishing Ltd, 1996.

ACKNOWLEDGMENTS

Author's acknowledgments

With very special thanks to David Redfern for his enthusiasm and for taking so many of these fabulous photographs, and to Nancy White for her patience and help; and to Will Steeds and Justina Leitão at Quadrillion for putting it all together.

To my editors past and present, who have allowed me to write about the music I love; and particularly John Aizlewood, Nick Coleman, Laura Lee Davies, Tony Herrington, Elaine Patterson, Bill Prince, Tony Russell and Dominic Wells. And to Richard Cook, without whom it wouldn't have happened.

And to my family – Malcolm, Claire and Lindsey – and my girlfriend Karen, for putting up with all the noise.

The ragtime piano interview appears in the following publications: Hasse, John Edward, ed. *Ragtime: its History, Composers and Music*. New York: Schirmer Books, 1985.

Campbell, James, ed. *The Picador Book of Blues and Jazz*. London: Picador, 1995.

Quotations used at the opening of Chapters 2, 3, 5, 8 and 9 are from Crow, Campbell, Davis, Davis and Lock, respectively.

Publisher's acknowledgments

The Publishers would like to thank Richard Cook for his help at the beginning of this project, and also The Bridgewater Book Company for their initial design concepts.

The following photographers are all represented by Redferns The Music Picture Library, 7, Bramley Road, London W10 6SZ, UK: Bob Baker; Dave Bennett Files; Paul Bergen; Fin Costello; GEMS; Dany Gignoux; William Gottlieb; Tim Hall; Mick Hutson; Max Jones Files; Michael Linssen; Marc Marnie; Stuart Nicholson; Michael Ochs Archives; Andrew Putler; David Redfern; Ebet Roberts; Chuck Stewart; Peter Symes; Gai Terrell; Bob Willoughby.

All William P. Gottlieb photographs are supplied courtesy of The Library of Congress: Ira & Lenore S. Gershwin Fund.